ENRON
PROOF
YOUR
401(k)

Steps to Keep
Your Money Safe

ENRON

PROOF

YOUR

401(k)

Steps to Keep
Your Money Safe

By Crista Boyles
The 401(k) & Pension Coach™

TWIN LION PUBLISHERS
HOUSTON

Books are available for bulk purchases at special discounts. For information, please write the publisher at the above address.

Trademarked Words
This term in this book and on the book covers is trademarked by Crista Boyles: The 401(k) & Pension Coach.

First edition published 2003
10 9 8 7 6 5 4 3 2 1

Printed in the United States of America

Boyles, Crista.
   Enron proof your 401(k) : steps to keep your money
safe / by Crista Boyles.
   p. cm.
   Includes bibliographical references and index.
   ISBN 0-9723695-3-8

   1. 401(k) plans.   I. Title.

HD7105.45.U6B69 2002   332.024'01
                        QBI02-200614

To Millie Bynum

CONTENTS

PART 2
ESSENTIAL KNOWLEDGE TO PROTECT YOUR 401(K)

APPENDIXES

Acknowledgments

I am very fortunate to have had the assistance of a number of people in the completion of this book:

■ My wise, kind, and generous husband. I am very blessed to have a business partner, best friend, and husband, all rolled into one. His encouragement and sacrifice made this book possible.

■ Special thanks goes to Mardell Boyles for her comments, suggestions, and support. She went above and beyond the call of duty to assist me.

■ Thanks goes to Rob Collie for his suggestions for Chapter 1, comments, suggestions and support.

■ Special thanks to Lance Roberts for his quote on the back of the book.

■ For the contribution of their experience in working with Enron employees or employees with significant amounts of company stock: Paul Ferraresi, CFP®; Mark Gleason, CFA; Richard K. Hammel, CFP® and his daughter, Melissa Hammel; Timothy Hayes; Adam Hill, CFP®; Derek V. Irish, CFP®; George Middleton, CFA, CPA/PFS; Rob Moody, M.S., CFA, CFP®, CLU, ChFC; and, Pat Raskob.

■ My special thanks to the Communications Manager of The Vanguard Group, John Demming, for arranging an interview with F. William McNabb III, head of the Institutional Investor Group for The Vanguard Group.

Also special thanks to David Wray of the Profit Sharing/401(k) Council of America for an interview that provided excellent insights into the success of 401(k)s.

A big heart felt thanks to Delynn Halloran for her support, experience, and efforts to assist in the process of translating the manuscript into a book.

Appreciation to Gary Butler for his suggestions for Chapter 1, and support for this project.

I want to express my appreciation to each and everyone of our clients that have encouraged this project, or have provided me with experiences that contributed to this project.

I also want to take the opportunity to thank the many 401(k) participants that have read my columns and attended my workshops. Your comments, suggestions, questions, experiences and support have made this book possible.

■ I thank my mother for passing on to me the ability to view problems from new and creative perspectives, and for her enthusiasm for this book project.

I thank my dad for introducing me to the wonderful stories of Sherlock Holmes and Horatio Hornblower, who never gave up until they solved the mystery at hand with their own unique perspectives. Also for his encouragement with this project.

I appreciate Annelie Moxter-Collie's encouragement to accomplish this project.

And finally, my deepest thanks to God Almighty who moved heaven and earth to help me accomplish this book.

Warning: Disclaimer

This book is designed to provide information to help participants in 401(k)s to manage their 401(k) accounts. It's sold with the understanding that the publisher and author aren't engaged in rendering legal, accounting, financial planning, investment planning or other professional services. If legal or other expert assistance is required, the services of a competent professional should be sought.

It's not the purpose of this book to reprise all the information that is otherwise available to authors and/or publishers, but instead to amplify and supplement other texts. You're urged to read all the available material, and learn as much as possible about your corporate retirement plans, including 401(k) plans.

Every effort has been made to make this manual as accurate as possible. However, there may be mistakes, both typographical and in content. Therefore, this text should be used only as a general guide and not as the ultimate source of 401(k) information. Furthermore, this book contains information on 401(k)s and managing 401(k)s that is current only up to the printing date. Laws and regulations constantly change, and may have changed since the printing date.

The purpose of this book is to educate and entertain. The author and publisher shall have neither liability nor responsibility to any person or entity with respect to any loss or damage caused, or alleged to have been caused, directly or indirectly, by the information contained in this book.

If you don't wish to be bound by the above, you may return this book to the publisher for a refund of the purchase price.

INTRODUCTION

You can learn a lot from the terrible things that happened to the Enron employees and their 401(k)s. It's too late for them, but not for you. Reading this book and acting upon the principles in it could be the difference between a comfortable retirement or a nightmare.

Consider this book a hand-held consultant to guide you to 401(k) safety. This book is no academic treatise on 401(k)s, nor is it a substitute for the lengthy books on everything you didn't really want to know about 401(k) laws. If you want to learn the steps to keep your 401(k) safe – this is the book for you.

I help corporate employees with their 401(k)s for a living. It's thrilling to hear the success stories, like the employee who told me that I'd rescued his retirement by advising him just in the nick of time to sell his company stock and get in a safer investment. I'm delighted with the many attendees of my 401(k) workshops and readers of my "401(k) & Pension Coach™" column who finally understand their 401(k)s, and can now make better choices.

As I received stories from financial advisors around the country about how they had either helped Enron employees rescue their 401(k) money, or employees in other companies in similar situations, I have been struck with the importance of having a source for impartial advice. It's so easy for all of us to get wrapped up in the success of the moment, the thrill of seeing our 401(k) surge ahead as the company stock price climbs. But alas, it often ends in a bittersweet tale. What goes up can, and often does, come down.

The Enron tale is an amazing tale. Little of the true nature of the 401(k) disaster has reached the public. Now, you'll find out what really happened, and the secrets to keeping it from happening to you.

PART 1
WHAT
REALLY
HAPPENED
AT
ENRON ?

1   HOW THE ENRON
401(K) TRAGEDY
UNFOLDED

How do you Enron proof your 401(k)? If you have your money in a 401(k), you need to know the steps to take to protect your money. This book gives you those steps, and helps you understand what happened at Enron to destroy approximately two billion dollars of Enron employee retirement savings.

Here is the stripped-down Enron 401(k) story so you can see what happened, and learn to avoid the same fate.

Dangerous Illusion

A warning was issued by *Forbes* magazine in 1993 about the aggressive type of accounting Enron had switched to in 1991. The magazine predicted the result would likely lead to problems since this form of accounting initially boosts profits, but as the years roll by, it creates tremendous pressure on a company to continually sign up more business just to keep its head above water.

Catching a similar line of thinking, Carol Coale, noted analyst at Prudential Securities, downgraded Enron's stock the following year. She believed Enron would have difficulty meeting its earnings estimates. Jeffrey Skilling verbally lambasted her at an analyst meeting shortly after the downgrade.

Prior to 1994, Enron had been making regular contributions to the Enron Employee Stock Ownership Plan (ESOP) on behalf of each Enron employee who met the qualifications to be a participant. Beginning in 1994, Enron began allowing employees who met certain criteria to move their money out of the ESOP, which only had Enron stock as an investment, and into the Enron 401(k), which had a variety of investment choices. In 1994 and 1995, Enron made a few contributions to the ESOP and then stopped, shifting the focus of the employees' corporate retirement savings to the Enron 401(k). Millions of dollars of Enron employee money would slowly be transferred out of the Enron ESOP over the next few years.

In December 1999, someone asked at an Enron all-employee meeting, "Should we invest all our 401(k) in Enron stock?" "Absolutely," answered the woman leader at the front of the room. It's all caught on video tape. (The woman is identified as "Cindy" on the tape. The President of Enron, Jeffrey Skilling, is apparently agreeing with her, and Ken Lay, Enron's CEO, can be seen nearby.) The Enron stock price was approximately $44 per share.

Accolades were heaped on the company by the media, even Enron's Chief Financial Officer, Andrew Fastow, won an

4

award sponsored by Arthur Anderson (the auditing firm for Enron) from *CFO* magazine. Based on a survey, *Fortune* magazine labeled Enron, "The Most Innovative Company in America," and placed it 24th on the list of the, "100 Best Companies to Work for in America." *The Financial Times* awarded Enron, "Energy Company of the Year." *BusinessWeek* magazine lauded Jeffrey Skilling by including him in the, "e.biz 25," the top twenty-five Internet movers and shakers in the world. By August of the year 2000, Enron was one of the darlings of Wall Street. Its stock hit $90.56. Enron executives talked about the stock price going to $100 or $120 per share.

A month later, however, in the Texas Regional section of *The Wall Street Journal* an article by Jonathan Weil cast doubt on Enron's accounting practices. In a video-taped Enron employees' meeting, Jeffrey Skilling assured the employees the particular technique the newspaper was assailing was right and proper.

The Wall Street Journal article caught the eye of noted short-seller and hedge fund manager, Jim Chanos, who dug into Enron's financials. He believed that his initial study revealed Enron stock was very overpriced due to what he thought looked like shady accounting. He began to *short* Enron stock. (An investor makes money shorting a stock when the stock's price goes down.)

Nell Minow, noted shareholder-rights advocate, spoke to the National Association of Corporate Directors in October

2000. She warned them that the Enron board of directors might not be paying attention to the company as they should.

As the year 2000 closed, Enron stock was soaring at $83.13 per share, but a nasty slide was about to begin.

Cindy Olson, who many believe is the "Cindy" who appeared in the December 1999 Enron video, sold $6.5 million of Enron stock at the end of 2000 and beginning of 2001 on the advice of her financial advisor. According to Olson, he counseled her to diversify her investments.

Jeffrey Skilling became CEO in February of 2001, and Ken Lay, age 59, agreed to remain as chairman of the board until 2005 in order to groom a successor.

More doubts were expressed about Enron's financial health. In early 2001, when Jim Chanos announced his belief that Enron would implode, other hedge-fund managers began helping him unravel the mysteries of Enron's financial reports. Bethany McLean in *Fortune* magazine's March 5 issue, wrote of grave doubts about Enron's stock and believed it to be over-priced. TheStreet.com published a sell recommendation on Enron stock by analyst, Mark Roberts. On July 25, Peter Worden, of TC2000 charting software, issued a warning on Enron stock, which was now around $54.00 per share.

In the early spring, Enron began the hunt for a new trustee for its 401(k) plan to replace the current trustee, Northern Trust Company. (Enron stated in late 2001, that the Enron 401(k) plan administration committee was trying to upgrade the Enron

401(k) by bringing in a new trustee.) The company solicited bids from third-party benefits firms. Hewitt Associates was tapped as the new Enron 401(k) trustee in July, 2001. Plans moved forward for the transition of the 401(k) from Northern Trust to Hewitt. The transfer of Enron 401(k) participant assets and records would require one month, a standard length for the industry.

Enron enterprises failed one after another during the first six months of 2001. With each successive deal going sour, the Enron stock price slumped lower. The Blockbuster deal was called off. Enron's expensive power plant deal in India was failing. Enron's Azurix water company failed and was being sold off in pieces. Enron's off-the-books partnerships were written so that if Enron's credit ever went to junk bond status, then enormous amounts of debt would be passed from the partnerships to the corporation. If a company's stock price slips too low, this can cause the credit rating services to lower the company's credit rating. Enron's stock price had fallen by over 40% by August, 2001. Many believe there is no mystery why Jeffrey Skilling departed.

On August 14, Jeffrey Skilling resigned and left Enron with $67 million. He was Enron's President and CEO for six months. Ken Lay assumed his former position of CEO and continued his position as chairman of the board. He promised Wall Street more transparency with earnings. Wall Street didn't take kindly to the departure of Enron's chief visionary, sending Enron stock 6% lower to a level not seen in more than eighteen months: $40.25. The stock had lost approximately 50% of its value since the previous December.

On the day Skilling left, Lay sent an upbeat, positive e-mail to all Enron employees stating his confidence in the company and its future.

Shortly after Jeffrey Skilling left, Enron Vice President Sherron Watkins sent an anonymous, seven page memo to Ken Lay detailing the accounting disaster she believed could unfold at Enron. Watkins is an ex-Arthur Andersen CPA. She was working as senior manager of corporate development for Andrew Fastow, and had gotten a good look at the company's accounting.

A few days later, Watkins alerted Cindy Olson, Enron executive for human resources, that Enron may have an impending accounting disaster overwhelm the corporation. Olson, a member of the committee that oversaw the Enron 401(k), didn't alert the other Enron 401(k) plan administration officials about Watkins's assertions. She arranged a meeting for Watkins with Ken Lay. Watkins also contacted Arthur Andersen and stated her serious concerns about Fastow's partnerships.

Just after midnight a few days later, Chung Wu, a UBS PaineWebber broker in Houston, e-mailed dozens of clients who were Enron employees telling them to consider selling Enron stock because he believed Enron had financial troubles. Enron sharply complained to Wu's branch manager who sent a rebuttal e-mail to the dozens of Enron employees Wu had contacted.

Wu was fired. (As a side note, UBS PaineWebber rated Enron stock a "strong buy" until four days before Enron's bankruptcy.)

The same week as Wu's firing, Sherron Watkins had her first face-to-face meeting with Ken Lay about her accounting allegations. They had at least two more follow-up meetings. (She later testified before a congressional committee that she felt he took her concerns very seriously, but simply didn't comprehend the magnitude of the accounting irregularities.) Watkins recommended that the law firm of Vinson & Elkins, an outside law firm Enron frequently used, not be used to investigate her claims because they were already heavily involved with other Enron projects. Lay, nevertheless, decided to use Vinson & Elkins to investigate her allegations.

Sherron Watkins, in her congressional testimony months later, recounted how she felt Andrew Fastow's fury when he discovered she had gone to Lay with her allegations. He wanted to confiscate her computer and fire her. Watkins consulted with Cindy Olson, moved her files to a laptop, and handed over her computer to Fastow. Watkins also detailed to a congressional committee the environment of intimidation and fear Skilling and Fastow built at Enron. She stated that it was often said in the corridors of Enron, "Heads, Mr. Fastow wins; tails, Enron loses."

On August 23, Enron was downgraded from a "buy" to a "neutral" by BNP Paribas analyst Daniel Scotto, the lone analyst at this point to do so.

9

401(k) Disaster

A s the Enron stock price continued to descend, Ken Lay received e-mails from concerned Enron employees in late August and early September asking whether they should still be investing in Enron stock. Reportedly, he encouraged them to continue owning the stock.

On September 26, Ken Lay conducted an electronic town hall meeting with the Enron employees. The transcript of the meeting reveals that he spoke confidently about Enron and Enron stock. Lay told employees the stock was a bargain at $27.00. He also said the Enron third quarter results should be great. An employee specifically asked about the off-the-books partnerships, and the transcript says Lay assured the employees the external auditor and all internal officers believed they were appropriate and legal. (The law firm who released the transcript of the meeting, notes that Sherron Watkins was considered an internal officer.)

Some Portland General Electric employees claim that without warning, starting the same day as the electronic town hall meeting, they couldn't transfer to new investments in their Enron 401(k) accounts. At this time, Enron stock was a little above $25.

On October 4, Enron says it notified all 401(k) participants of the transition to the third-party administrator to begin on October 29. Over the next few weeks, Enron says that several e-mail notices were sent to Enron 401(k) participants reminding them of the upcoming "lockdown" period when no changes in investment selection would be able to be made because the 401(k) assets and records would be in transit.

(A number of accusations have been made concerning the "lockdown" and notices. One lawsuit filed by Enron 401(k) participants claims some Enron 401(k) participants who were no longer employees didn't receive any notice of the "lockdown." One of the lawsuits has a copy of an Enron announcement stating all requests to buy or sell in the 401(k) accounts must be in by October 26. Also, one of the lawsuits filed against Enron for 401(k) losses states that for some Enron 401(k) participants the "lockdown" was planned to begin on October 19, and that they couldn't access their accounts after that date. One law firm states that Enron sent out an inaccurate memo stating the "lockdown" would begin October 19, when it didn't actually begin until October 29, causing employees to think they couldn't sell their Enron stock when in actual fact they could have.)

On October 15, the law firm of Vinson & Elkins reported back to Ken Lay that no additional inquiry was needed to look into allegations of Enron accounting irregularities made by Sherron Watkins.

On October 16, Ken Lay announced to analysts an Enron write-off for restructuring charges and investment losses of $1.01 billion producing a third quarter loss of $618 million.

11

The losses were attributed to investments that went belly-up in retail energy sales, a disastrous foray into the water business and telecommunications. He briefly mentioned a $1.2 billion charge and stated that it wouldn't impact the credit rating of the corporation. Most analysts thought he meant the previously mentioned billion dollar charge, and pressed for more details. The next day, Ken Lay refused questions, but finally, cryptically said the $1.2 billion write-down was related to failed investments. Analysts who were curious before, were now furious. Enron discounted the complaints, further exacerbating the escalating problem.

Moments after the announcement, Moody's credit rating service, placed on hold Enron's $13 billion in debt; followed shortly by the SEC privately asking Enron for information. Enron's death march had started.

Enron released word on October 22 that the SEC had requested information on the company's situation a few days before. Wall Street analysts were furious that Enron hadn't let them know immediately. Enron's stock price sank over 20%. The next day, Andersen's Chief Auditor for Enron, David Duncan, began a fourteen day document destruction of Enron related materials. The following day, Andrew Fastow was put on leave of absence by Enron.

By now, Enron employees were frantically e-mailing and begging Enron for the planned "lockdown" period to be abandoned. Despite the frantic calls, the "lockdown" of the

Enron 401(k) proceeded. (Enron insists it began on October 29. One of the 401(k) participants' lawsuits states the "lockdown" began October 26.) The Enron stock price was $13.81.

Treasury Secretary Paul O'Neill answered his telephone on October 29 and found Ken Lay on the other end asking him for help. O'Neill didn't oblige. Two days later, the downgrading of Enron's credit status was begun by credit rating agencies, which sounded Enron's death knell.

On November 8, Enron stunned an already shaken Wall Street when it released the news that it would restate earnings all the way back to 1997. Again, Ken Lay telephoned Treasury Secretary Paul O'Neill, but O'Neill declined assistance since he believed an Enron failure would have little affect on the financial markets.

Also on November 8, Robert Rubin, the former Treasury Secretary in the Clinton Administration, now chairman of Citigroup's executive committee, telephoned an undersecretary in the Treasury. Rubin requested he contact the credit-rating agencies to mediate for Enron. The undersecretary rejected this request. (Later in 2002, allegations came to light accusing Citigroup and Rubin with helping Enron create a ruse to hide enormous amounts of Enron's debt. The *Washington Times* has speculated that if Enron's debt hadn't been downgraded, this possible ruse may not have been revealed.)

On November 10, Enron snapped up Dynegy's billion dollar buy-out offer. Enron stock rose slightly to $8.63. Ken Lay agreed to leave Enron as part of the Dynegy deal. The crisis appeared over.

According to Enron the "lockdown" ended on November 12, and on November 13 participants were free to move out of Enron stock. This means the "lockdown," according to Enron, lasted only ten trading days (days when the stock markets are open, and stock can be bought and sold). Enron's stock price was just under $10.00 on November 13. (One of the lawsuits filed by Enron 401(k) participants claims the "lockdown" wasn't completed until November 14, and that Hewitt, the new trustee, announced the end of the "lockdown" on that day.) The first Enron 401(k) participant lawsuit was filed just after the "lockdown" ended.

Enron stock by now had tumbled to $10.00 from a high of $90.56. Out of the fifteen stock analysts that followed Enron, more than 50% of them were still rating it a "buy" or better at this time, which prompted CNNMoney to express a lack of appreciation for stock analysts.

Just before Thanksgiving an ex-Enron vice president, who was laid off a few months earlier, made a hardship withdrawal request from the Enron deferred compensation plan, of about $200,000. He needed the funds for a family emergency. When he didn't hear anything from Enron, he called, but made no progress in receiving his money. Meanwhile, his friends who were also in the Enron deferred compensation plan, but were still employed by the company, were receiving their money, sometimes within twenty-four hours. Other ex-employees in the deferred compensation plan were having similar frustrations. (Months later the plan administrator's attorney confirmed that during this period of time current employees received their money and ex-employees didn't.)

On November 22, Enron's stock sunk even lower and closed at $5.01.

On November 28, the final nail was put in Enron's coffin as Enron's credit rating was downgraded by three leading rating agencies to junk bond status, which resulted in $3.9 billion in debt coming due right away. Enron's stock price plummeted 85%. Dynegy quickly backed away from the merger in light of Enron's crushing debt load. Suddenly, the business which had produced 90% of Enron's earnings, the online trading system, shut down. The players in the energy market were caught off guard. U.S. energy regulators kept a pulse on the emergency, but noted few disruptions in the market.

Enron's stock price slipped below $1.00 on November 28 and was removed from the prestigious S&P 500® stock market index at the close of trading. Later the Enron stock price cratered 45% to hit 36 cents as the large institutional S&P 500® mutual funds had to divest of Enron stock. Amazingly, it was still rated a "buy" or "strong buy" by four stock analysts.

Just days before Enron filed for bankruptcy, $55 million was paid to executives and top management for retention bonuses.

Enron filed Chapter 11 bankruptcy on December 2. It was the largest reorganization bankruptcy in world history to that date. Energy markets around the world shuddered. Enron laid off approximately 4,000 employees out of 21,000. The Enron Vice President of Corporate and Enterprise Systems, Allan Sommer, gutted out laying off 350 employees, then got his pink slip a few days later.

Much to the frustration of angry Enron 401(k) participants, the bankruptcy filing temporarily protected Enron from lawsuits. Enron 401(k) participants were further enraged when Enron received its request for the bankruptcy case to be heard in New York, not Houston. (The law allowed Enron, to a large degree, to determine where the bankruptcy case would be heard.)

Court Wars

Just after the new year began, the U.S. Justice Department released information that an Enron criminal investigation had commenced.

A few days later, the New York Stock Exchange halted the trading of Enron stock, and dropped it from the trading list. The next day, the Enron stockholders received a final affront as Enron stock was delisted from the NASDAQ stock exchange and began to be offered on the bulletin boards known as "pink sheets" that sometimes offer fraudulent penny stocks.

In a January 20 article, the *Houston Chronicle* revealed Andrew Fastow was receiving death threats. He was, at that time, a defendant in over forty shareholder and Enron employee lawsuits filed in the previous three months.

Combing meticulously through Enron's financial records, investigators uncovered an intricate web of deals with over 3,000 firms and over $5 billion in Enron's investments and loans that were made over the last few years. It's unclear where all the money went.

On January 23, Ken Lay resigned as chief executive of Enron, and resigned from the board two weeks later.

In a bizarre 401(k) twist, a deed transfer for Ken and Linda Lay's million dollar Galveston home arrived at the Galveston County Clerk's office. The deed transfer stated the ownership of the home was transferred to the "Enron 401(k) Employee Trust." An alert county clerk ascertained it was phony. The Lays denied they executed the deed.

On January 28, Enron ex-employees went to court in an attempt to win back some of their lost millions from Enron top executives, Andersen and other firms involved with the Enron collapse.

On February 5, testifying before the Senate Governmental Affairs Committee, Cindy Olson, explained how she encouraged Enron employees to diversify and had financial advisors come in for employee brown bag lunch seminars. Congressman Waxman alerted the committee's Chairman that her statements appeared to not be completely accurate, and turned over the December 1999 video tape of the all-employee meeting in which it appears that Olson was encouraging Enron employees to have a high percentage of their 401(k)s in Enron stock.

Before a Senate committee, a former Enron employee explained his feelings about the collapse, "I now understand why people jumped out of windows during the Great Depression." He appealed to Congress to declare the top company officials personally liable for the employees' losses.

Enron's benefits manager, Mikie Rath, denied allegations before a House hearing that an employee benefits account had money diverted to other uses.

Jeffrey Skilling testified that he never knew of anything improper about the partnerships. He stated, "It was my understanding that the purpose of the transactions was to provide a real hedge." Skilling further stated that when he resigned in August of last year, "I absolutely, unequivocally thought the company was in good shape." Skilling was questioned closely about significant events, but said he couldn't recall.

On February 12, the Labor Department announced it would endeavor to replace Enron's retirement plan officials with an independent expert skilled in looking out for the interests of participants.

On Valentine's Day, Carolyn Schwartz, the U.S. trustee in the Enron bankruptcy case, announced she would take the extraordinary step of giving ex-employees their own committee at the request of Texas Attorney General John Cornyn. The new committee would have equal standing with the already established creditors committee and would give ex-employees clout. Enron was required to pick up the tab for legal fees and expenses associated with the new committee.

On February 20, a victory for Enron 401(k) participants occurred when Judge Arthur Gonzales of the U.S. Bankruptcy Court of the Southern District of New York set the future date for when the stay against Enron litigation would be lifted, so Enron 401(k) participants' lawsuits could move forward. At the same time, he ordered Enron to allow plaintiffs' lawyers access to certain documents. Another victory – the case would be tried in Houston, not New York.

In a startling announcement, the government reported that the Enron pension plan was underfunded, and the government might take over the plan. The pension plan was underfunded to the tune of $125 million or more. Assets at the time of the announcement were approximately $220 million with an estimated 20,000 pension participants in the plan. No missed benefit payments to retirees occurred prior to the announcement date.

Laid-off Enron workers, who still hadn't received their full severance pay, were infuriated when they learned that over a two-year period prior to Enron's collapse, bonuses and payments to approximately two thousand Enron corporate executives totaled an amazing $432 million. Especially, infuriating

19

was the $55 million in retention bonuses paid just prior to the bankruptcy.

On March 14, State Street Bank was named as the independent fiduciary of the Enron traditional defined-benefit plan, 401(k), and ESOP by the U.S. Labor Department. The Labor Department further noted that Enron agreed to pay the fees for the independent fiduciary rather than the current trend toward the fees being deducted from the plans in an attempt to spare as much money in the plans as possible for participants. The plan quickly ran into trouble when the creditor committee objected to Enron paying the fee of the trustee for the retirement plans with corporate money instead of it being paid by the plan participants.

In federal court on April 8, a consolidated complaint was filed accusing nine banks of false sales, bank executives of a "Ponzi scheme," law firms of phony deals, and executives of insider trading. The banks read like a who's who of the banking industry: J.P. Morgan Chase, Lehman Brothers, Deutsche Bank, Citigroup, Merrill Lynch, Bank America, Credit Suisse First Boston, and Canadian Imperial Bank of Commerce. (If attorneys for Enron's creditors can succeed in tracing the fraud trail into the banks, then the money spigot could be turned on and creditors, including Enron 401(k) participants, might recover substantial amounts of money.)

Portland General Electric employees, some of whom lost large sums in Enron stock in their Enron 401(k)s, received an unexpected blow when they discovered that through "dead peasant" life insurance policies, their deaths will enrich Enron executives running their company. The life insurance policies are allowed in a majority of states, and in this particular case, go to replenish the cost of executive retirement plans. Portland General insists their employees signed the appropriate forms for consent, but judging by the employees reaction, it must have been in verrry fine print!

On May 3, the reorganization plan was announced for Enron, which included the goal to sell Enron to one buyer. The company would be stripped to essentials and returned to its roots with $11 billion in power plants, pipelines, and electricity transport and have twelve thousand employees in South, Central and North America. The temporary new name was OpCo.

On June 21, the stay against Enron lawsuits lifted, and Enron 401(k) participants' legal case against Enron began to move forward.

Cindy Olson, Enron executive for human resources, announced she would be resigning as of July 15.

Americans began to take a humorous look at Enron. *Playbill* announced that *Professional Skepticism*, a rollicking new comedy set in a Big Five accounting firm would burst on a New England stage July 3. Written by a former accountant with a Big Five firm, it would take a comedic look at accounting abuses at large corporations. The tongue-in-cheek news release for the play poked fun at Ken Lay and Jeffrey Skilling. The fun continued elsewhere in the country with a baseball team having a shredding night to "honor" Arthur Andersen. Attendees of the game were urged to bring documents to shred at shredding stations located throughout the stadium.

2 THE REAL STORY OF THE ENRON 401(K)

Lawyers will have a knock-down-drag-out brawl in court over what laws Enron management may have trampled. Enron management is accused of terrible things, but there are lessons to be learned that can result in you navigating your 401(k) away from a similar disaster.

As with most large U.S. companies, Enron had more than just the 401(k) in its retirement and compensation plan arsenal. There appears to have been at least six Enron plans Enron employees lost money in:

■ The Enron Corporation Savings Plan, which is the 401(k) you've heard about.

■ The Enron Employee Stock Ownership Plan (ESOP), which almost completely contained Enron company stock. As you can imagine, this plan was slaughtered as a result of the Enron stock dive.

■ The Cash Balance Plan, which is a newer type of pension that is portable, similar to 401(k)s. Because of unique connections to the Enron stock, it has been included in the consolidated Enron 401(k) participants' lawsuit. In 1996, it replaced the Enron Corporation Retirement Plan, a traditional pension program.

■ The Enron stock option plan. A corporate stock option plan generally allows participants in the plan to buy or sell a certain number of shares of company stock at a specified price until a certain date.

■ The "phantom stock" plan in which Enron matched a certain percentage of the employees' salary in stock and the stock was available to employees only after a certain number of years. This was a "bookkeeping only" type of plan in which the company simply records that an employee can have such-and-such an amount in so many years. There are no real assets in these types of plans, unlike 401(k) plans which do.

■ A management deferred compensation plan estimated to have had four hundred participants. Typically, these type of deferred compensation plans are set up to give managers and executives above a certain salary level a way to save for retirement after they have maxed out the amount the law allows to be contributed to their 401(k)s. These types of programs are also a "bookkeeping only" program.

24

It helps clear up some confusion in stories that you may have heard if you know that there was more than one plan that the Enron employees lost money in. Most people assume the employees' losses were just in the Enron 401(k) because that has been the focus of most media stories. A careful review of the reported losses in the Enron 401(k) participants' consolidated lawsuit, however, reveals the losses were spread around in each of these six plans (depending on the individual). It doesn't reduce how terrible the losses were, but this information can give you a better understanding of the situation.

The Enron retirement and compensation plans fall into two groups which are: those protected from bankruptcy and those that weren't. ESOP and 401(k) participant assets aren't considered company assets, and so they are protected if the sponsoring company goes bankrupt. Pension plans are insured by a special government program, so pension plan assets are protected to a certain extent. The deferred compensation plan and the "phantom stock" program weren't protected from the bankruptcy. They are considered unsecured debt in a bankruptcy, so there normally is little hope for a recovery of losses.

Enron's Handling of the 401(k) and ESOP

T he lawsuits by 401(k) participants accuse Enron management of a number of things. Some involving the 401(k) and

ESOP you've heard repeatedly in the media, but others have barely received a whisper outside of law offices.

Giving False Information

The following is either what Enron management has been accused of in some of the lawsuits, or has been accused of in the media. As of publication, no Enron court trial had occurred.

■ Concealing billions of dollars in debt which, when finally revealed, caused the price of Enron stock to collapse.

■ Stating publicly a confident belief in Enron stock while selling it like crazy in secret.

■ Accounting trickery and sleight of hand that would have amazed even Houdini.

■ A "pattern of racketeering activity" by Enron's top executives, Arthur Andersen, certain investment banks, and certain law firms participating in the schemes and conspiracies.

■ That the financial chicanery of this group of executives, companies, banks, and law firms resulted in their being enriched by hundreds of millions of dollars while skewering investors.

■ That Enron top executives created a vast conspiracy to pump up the Enron stock price while they looted the company at the expense of the 401(k) participants.

■ Obstruction of justice by both Enron and Arthur Andersen.

■ That Enron and Arthur Andersen were aware they were certifying false financial documents, and this false and misleading information led the Enron 401(k) participants to purchase or hold Enron stock.

■ The value of the Enron stock paid as company match to the Enron employees wasn't the value it was represented to be. Along with this, is an accusation that the way Enron saved itself money with the company match resulted in top management's being able to pay out lavish salaries.

Being Lousy ERISA Fiduciaries

ERISA is an acronym for the primary body of law governing 401(k)s, ESOPs, and many similar plans. Under ERISA, certain people associated with a company's 401(k) plan administration are considered fiduciaries.

According to ERISA, a fiduciary has "the duty to act with the care, skill, prudence, and diligence under the prevailing circumstances that a prudent person with like knowledge and like capacity would use to conduct an enterprise of like character with like aims." In other words, they should do the right thing with your money. There is little argument that there are strong feelings the fiduciaries at Enron didn't do this.

Another thing 401(k) fiduciaries are required to do is to be loyal to the plan rather than the company who sponsors the plan. They are to "act solely in the participants' interest and for the exclusive purpose of providing benefits to them." Cindy Olson, Enron's executive for human resources and a member of the committee overseeing the 401(k), is thought by many to have violated this principle by not taking action to alert Enron 401(k) participants to a problem with Enron stock after Sherron Watkins stated her allegations to Olson in August of 2001. Olson, on her part, contends she took the proper steps by making arrangements for Watkins to take the problem to Ken Lay, and she knew Lay started an investigation into the allegations.

In addition to the above, 401(k) fiduciaries are required to operate the 401(k) plan in accordance with the rules of the plan, but are to throw away the rule book if following the plan rules would violate the duties of loyalty to the participants and/or prudence. Many Enron 401(k) participants strongly feel the committee who oversaw the Enron 401(k) should have stepped outside of the rules, halted plans for the "lockdown," and taken other strong measures to put the interest of the 401(k) participants first.

Along with this, the 401(k) participants' consolidated lawsuit contends the committee should have blocked the "lockdown" from proceeding.

Failure to Jump Through All Documentation Hoops

One of the 401(k) participants' lawsuits claims Enron didn't supply the 401(k) participants with a proper prospectus for the Enron stock so their purchases should be rescinded. (A prospectus is a formal document informing an investor of what they need to know to make a buying decision.)

Over Promotion of Company Stock Ownership

This group of accusations is based on the general business assumption that management is benefited by a large block of company stock being in the friendly, stable hands of employees, and because the ownership of company stock motivates employees. Enron's executives are accused of having gone overboard in promoting Enron stock, and knowingly promoted an unsafe and falsely priced investment for their benefit to the detriment of the employees:

■ Enron didn't make sure employees age 50 and over clearly understood they could sell their company match upon reaching the age of 50. It's acknowledged, however, that the Summary Plan Description for the Enron 401(k) did state this information. (A Summary Plan Description is a formal booklet required by law that explains the 401(k) plan rules to the participants.)

■ Enron didn't make sure employees were warned of the dangers of owning an extremely high percentage of company stock in their retirement portfolios. Cindy Olson stated to one of the congressional committees investigating Enron that the 401(k) plan administration committee had tried to communicate the dangers of being undiversified. Shortly after her testimony, a 1999 video tape came to light in which a person named "Cindy" is encouraging employees to own a high level of Enron stock in their 401(k)s.

■ Enron management strongly promoted company stock ownership to employees as a way to support the company, and also promoted it as a valuable benefit.

■ The 401(k) plan administration committee sought the advice of consultants about the suitability of the mutual funds in the 401(k), but had no objective procedures to review the suitability of Enron stock being offered as an investment option in the 401(k).

■ The committee also is accused of allowing top management to influence it to not terminate the company match in Enron stock.

The "Lockdown": Bad Timing and Bad Errors

Many Enron 401(k) participants are furious because Enron proceeded with the "lockdown" when damaging financial disclosures had just been made about the company, and the stock was falling in price. Many strongly feel the "lockdown" should have been canceled. Enron has stated that it would have been extremely difficult to have stopped the scheduled transition from taking place, which had been in the planning stages since July 2001.

In addition, both Cindy Olson and James Prentice, the head of the 401(k) plan administration committee, have asked how were they to know what was going to happen to the stock price? When I first read these types of statements in the media, my first reaction was probably the same as a lot of people, "Well, that's reallllly stupid." When presented in the media as naked statements hanging out there with no stock market data with it – and everyone knows the outcome

– it does look really dumb. It took me a moment to realize, hey, big company stocks do fall off cliffs and later recover.

Large and prestigious companies have experienced precipitous drops in their stock prices and the companies haven't gone bankrupt. Some of these companies and their stock price drops are: Lockheed Martin $58 to $17 (recently recovered to $65); Con Edison from $18 to $3; Sears Roebuck from $61 to $15; IBM $170 to $37; Xerox $60 to $6; to name just a few. This has also happened to some "A" rated bonds of powerful companies such as GM, Ford, and Citicorp, which went from $1000 to $490, etc.

Now, with all the other factors thrown in, whether the Enron 401(k) plan administration committee should have pulled the Enron company stock from the 401(k) or postponed the "lockdown" will have to be decided in court.

Travis B. Fuller, whose office was within sight of the Enron building, throws an interesting light on the problem, "Word on the street during the "lockdown" wasn't that Enron employees wanted to sell, it was that they wanted to buy. The employees thought the stock price was at a bargain-basement price, and they could make some quick money."

When the Enron disaster happened, it at first appeared the "lockdown" had been fabricated as a scheme to prop up the Enron stock price long enough for top executives to sell their stock. This seems to have been dispelled as evidence has come to light the Enron committee had been working on the transition for months. One of the lawsuits does, however, include a statement that having shares of Enron stock tied up in the 401(k) and the ESOP meant these couldn't be readily sold, and permitted top executives to unload their own Enron stock held outside of the 401(k) plan.

The impression left from some media stories is that Enron executives were able to sell their Enron stock when employees couldn't. The implication most people carry away from these stories is there was something unfair going on in the Enron 401(k). Enron has released a statement that all employees, including executives, were barred from selling in the 401(k) during the "lockdown" period. The confusion appears to be caused by the executives' ability to sell stock in other retirement and compensation plans (such as stock options) that weren't affected by the 401(k)'s "lockdown."

Some 401(k) participants who work for Portland General Electric in Oregon claim they were frozen out of their Enron 401(k)s as early as late September even though the "lockdown" was officially not to begin until October 29. Other participants report they were barred from selling as of October 19.

Some ex-Enron employees state they didn't receive any notification of the "lockdown."

Quirks in the Enron 401(k) and ESOP Plans

The Enron 401(k) Plan

If I were to ask shoppers randomly in any mall in America if the Enron 401(k) is still operating, I'd probably be told it's shut down, trashed, and long gone. In reality, Enron employees are still contributing, and the mutual fund investments in it are almost completely unaffected by the tragedy.

What You May Not Know About the Enron 401(k)

The Enron 401(k) was your basic, run-of-the mill 401(k) plan typically offered by large U.S. companies.

What investments were available in the Enron 401(k)? You may be very surprised to learn that it's not true, as has been suggested in some accounts of the disaster, that Enron offered only Enron stock in the Enron 401(k).

The typical 401(k) plan offers about fourteen investment selections. Enron's plan offered twenty in its 401(k). There were eighteen mutual funds and two company stock funds. According to David Wray of the Profit Sharing/401(k) Council of America, this is a larger number of fund options than is usually offered in 401(k) plans, even at large companies. The company stock funds were the Enron Corporate Stock Fund and another

34

stock fund that doesn't appear to be in dispute in the lawsuits. The Enron 401(k) participants' consolidated lawsuit states clearly that Enron 401(k) participants were always offered investments in the 401(k) that were appropriate for retirement contributions.

How much of the Enron employees' money was invested in Enron stock? One of the Enron 401(k) participants' lawsuits states that as of January 1, 2001, about 63% of the total assets in the Enron 401(k) and ESOP added together were invested in Enron stock. This means almost 40% of the total assets weren't in Enron stock and therefore didn't lose value in the Enron stock price crash.

Why did the Enron ESOP have big losses? Large corporate 401(k)s frequently have an Employee Stock Ownership Plan (ESOP) associated with them. An ESOP contains primarily company stock, except for a small portion held in cash or cash equivalents to handle daily redemptions. Large corporations find ESOPs (pronounced like "Aesop's" in Aesop's Fables) very useful for a variety of tax reasons and for use for corporate loans. It's also considered good business for both management and employees that a large body of company stock is held in friendly hands and not available to a hostile corporate raider (which was a problem in Enron's early history).

Federal regulations for ESOPs stipulate an employer must allow employees who are age 55 or older with ten years of service to sell up to 25% of their company stock each year.

35

Enron allowed employees aged 50 and older with five years of service to sell 20% of their company stock held in the Enron ESOP each year.

A portion of the compensation of full-time Enron employees between January 1, 1987 and December 31, 1994 was paid in Enron stock, which was placed in the Enron ESOP. Evidently for some corporate reason, Enron wasn't interested in continuing its ESOP plan. After 1994, new employees weren't included in the ESOP plan, and only dribbles of contributions were made to existing participants in 1995 and 1996. Gradually over the years, all participants who were age 50 or older and had been employed by Enron for a minimum of five years acquired the right to sell their Enron stock in the ESOP, so that by January 1, 2001 all participants aged 50 and older had acquired this right.

In fact, by January 1, 2001 it appears that about 60% of the assets had been transferred out. Therefore, a significant number of employees age 50 or older had sold off their Enron stock and transferred the money out. This was wise to do, since this retirement plan was no longer in favor with the company and because this plan had significant restrictions on moving the money from the plan.

Some retirees and others over age 50 had chosen not to transfer out of the ESOP. When the Enron stock crash occurred, the remaining ESOP participants were left with just pennies on the dollar. Any participants who were under age 50, weren't

permitted to move their money out of the ESOP. Those participants who were over age 50 and in the process of selling 20%
per year, weren't able to sell their Enron stock remaining in the
plan.

What were the number of Enron 401(k) participants?
The Enron 401(k) lawsuits don't agree, nor do the media reports, on how many people were participating in the plan when
the Enron stock price plunged. One says 11,000. One says
15,000. One says 24,000, but this last figure represents the four
largest Enron retirement plans lumped together.

**How much was lost by employees in the Enron 401(k)
and ESOP?** An Enron 401(k) or ESOP participant lost money
due to the sharp drop in the price of Enron stock. Keep in mind
the following losses mentioned represent the portion of the
participant's account invested in Enron stock. In most cases,
personal testimony indicates these individuals had elected to
keep 100% of their money in Enron stock.

One of the Enron 401(k) participants' lawsuits estimate
the losses on average to be a little less than $50,000 per partici-
pant. Two people are commonly cited by the media as losing
the most: $1.3 million and $1 million, respectively. Another case
often cited in the press is an employee who lost $700,000. Two
other employees are said to have lost $600,000 and $790,000,
respectively. In addition to these losses, the Enron 401(k) participants' lawsuits and congressional testimony list certain individuals as losing between $15,000 and $450,00. An attorney for

several 401(k) participants stated a figure around $450,000 as the maximum one of his clients had lost.

The total loss of Enron stock value in the Enron 401(k) and ESOP of approximately $2 billion occurred across a wide spectrum of the Enron employees. However, one of the 401(k) participants' lawsuits states that out of the total amount of Enron stock held in the Enron 401(k), 89% was from voluntary purchases. That means only 11% of the Enron stock in the 401(k) was company match that hadn't been sold. So, the vast majority of the Enron stock in the 401(k) didn't have any selling restriction on it, and was owned by choice.

Employees under age 50 had restrictions on selling the company match in the 401(k) or moving their money out of the ESOP. Even if employees under age 50 had wanted to diversify their Enron stock into a variety of investments in the 401(k), they couldn't have. They were stuck. It didn't matter if the Enron 401(k) was frozen or if the stock price was falling like a rock; they couldn't sell their Enron match or contribution in these two plans. Their voluntary purchases of Enron stock, however, could have been sold at any age.

The largest personal losses appear to have occurred in employees age 50 and older who had the right to sell their Enron match and move to other investments in the 401(k), but chose not to do so. Unfortunately, either few knew they could sell their company stock (which is very common nationally) or chose not to sell (which is also, unfortunately, very common).

I am a principal in a firm that is one of the only investment advisory firms in the country with a speciality in Lockheed Martin 401(k)s and pensions. A few years ago, our firm surmised Lockheed Martin's stock was very likely to be going down in the near future. The main 401(k) for Lockheed Martin doesn't allow the company match in company stock to be sold until an employee reaches age 55. We advised employees we knew who were allowed to sell their company stock to move their money to safer investments. We also advised those who had voluntarily purchased the company stock to do the same.

Those who took our advice were very grateful for it. Those that didn't, watched in stunned disbelief as the value of the stock descended from around $58 to $17. Many employees near retirement suffered by not selling their company stock. Some had to delay their long awaited retirement or retire on a fraction of what they had expected.

When we initially advised employees to sell their Lockheed Martin stock, their reactions were very interesting. In hindsight, it was similar to Noah telling everyone he knew to prepare for a flood when no one had ever seen rain before. It was very, very difficult for employees to comprehend their company stock might go down in value.

Why did Enron employees own so much Enron stock? In interview after interview, Enron 401(k) participants have stated Enron executives encouraged them to have all their 401(k) in company stock, and that executives not only stated it was a great investment, but that it was good for the company and showed company loyalty. Employees have stated they feel deeply betrayed by Enron executives.

3   EMPLOYEES WHO

RESCUED THEIR

MONEY

A little known secret in the Enron disaster is that some Enron employees rescued their money or a significant portion of it. So much emphasis has been put on the *loss* of money, that little coverage has gone to the Enron employees who *didn't* lose. Understanding how they were able to avoid losing their money can give you insight into how to keep your 401(k) money safe.

Good 401(k) Behavior

S ome of the Enron employees who didn't lose their money practiced what I refer to as "Good 401(k) Behavior."

They Followed Basic Financial Principles of Diversification in Managing Their 401(k) Accounts

An Enron employee in Houston had most of her retirement savings in Enron stock (approximately $600,000) as well as

Enron stock options. She turned for advice to Derek V. Irish, CFP® and client manager of Ronald Blue & Co., LLC. She was only in her 40's and couldn't sell the company match, but she was free to sell the vast majority of her Enron stock. She was taught about risk, the danger of owning too high a percentage of her net worth in company stock, and the value of diversifying away from owning company stock. She agreed to diversify her Enron 401(k) account and exercise some of the stock options. Instead of losing the majority of her savings in the Enron stock crash, she preserved 90% of her savings (approximately $520,000).

George S. Middleton, CFA, CPA/PFS of Limoges Investment Management was successful in assisting a client who worked for an Enron company. The client wasn't yet age 50 and couldn't sell his company match, but Middleton was able to work with the voluntary portion of the contributions. "I worked with a couple, and one of them had Enron company stock in his 401(k). I reviewed their situation and saw they needed to diversify. I encouraged them to do so. I spoke with them recently, and they are very happy they took my advice."

They Didn't Leave Money in Their Old 401(k) After Leaving the Company or Retiring

Some Enron employees retired and moved their money out of the Enron 401(k) before the stock debacle. They have been very quiet about the fact that they preserved their retirement money.

Adam was with Enron Europe, but left in September of 2001 to return to his family's farm in Scotland after years of working in London. Fortunately, he left at the right time, didn't leave his money in his retirement account at Enron, and cashed out of the company before he would have lost everything in Enron stock in his Enron retirement plans.

They Didn't Hold On to the Company Match

One of the 401(k) participants' lawsuits states that only 11% of the Enron 401(k) was company stock held because it was company match. That seems to mean to me that some people who were over age 50 were selling their company match. If they were selling their company match, then it's unlikely they were voluntarily buying Enron stock in their 401(k) accounts. Remember, only about 63% of the Enron 401(k) was held in Enron stock. Seems like some people were being very, very smart and keeping their ownership of company stock low. These individuals would have preserved the majority of their retirement funds at Enron when the company stock crashed.

They Rebalanced Their 401(k) Accounts

Some Enron employees who didn't lose their money used a technique called "rebalancing." They would systematically adjust the amount of company stock they owned by selling it, and diversifying into other investments in the 401(k).

Paul Ferraresi, CFP®, had four Enron employees as clients who had Enron stock in their Enron 401(k)s, and also held Enron stock options. The clients were enamored with Enron stock and its growth, so they weren't eager to reduce their holdings. Ferraresi, however, was able to develop a plan with each of his Enron clients so each one had an agreed on percentage of Enron company stock ownership they wouldn't go above in their 401(k) accounts. Any time one of the Enron client's company stock amount became too high, the client would sell off some shares to restore the balance between the Enron and non-Enron investments in his or her 401(k) account. This helped reduce the clients' losses when the Enron stock tumbled.

Good Investor Behavior

S ome Enron employees who didn't lose their money displayed good investor behavior.

They Didn't Rely On Company Executives' Public Statements Urging Employees to Hold Large Amounts of Company Stock

A misconception is that all Enron employees were convinced by management they should invest all their 401(k) money in Enron stock, and did so. What Enron management is accused of doing is truly shocking, but the reality is some of the employees ignored what the top executives were recommending.

One of the 401(k) lawsuits states 63% of the total assets in the 401(k) and the ESOP were in Enron stock. Where was the other 37%? It was in the other investment choices in the 401(k) plan. The full value of this portion was almost completely unaffected by the Enron collapse. The portion of a person's account that wasn't invested in Enron stock wasn't lost. A little known fact, is that any Enron employee aged 50 and over whose investment selection in the Enron 401(k) was diversified into any of the eighteen non-Enron stock investment options available in the Enron 401(k) lost very little during the plunge of Enron stock.

An Enron manager had a bad experience with one of the top Enron executives and was very concerned about being fired. This motivated her to meet with a financial advisor. The advisor noted most of her net worth was in Enron stock, and counseled her to reduce this dramatically. She did so. When Enron stock dramatically fell in late 2001, a very high percentage of her retirement money was saved from disaster.

They Didn't Hold On to the Company Stock That Had Fallen in an Attempt to Get Back Their Money

One of the signs of mature investors is that they cut their losses and sell losers. One of the signs of amateur investors is the opposite, they doggedly hold on to a stock wanting to make their money back in it before they sell it. It's one of the strongest behavioral tendencies in investing.

Even though most of the employees whose stories are told in this chapter aren't mature investors, they did a very smart thing. They turned to experienced, qualified financial professionals who could apply tested financial principles with third-party impartiality. These professionals were able to steer their clients away from this strong investor behavioral pattern. Even though Enron stock was falling during 2001, the advisors applied disciplined financial principles and recommended selling the falling stock.

They Sold Company Stock That Had Gone Up In Value and Took Their Profit

CFP® professional, Adam T. Hill, vice president of Maxwell Financial Management in Columbus, Ohio began advising Enron clients in early 2001, while the stock was still near $84, that it was time to take their profit in the stock and diversify. One of his clients, a company sales manager at Enron's local facility, was heavily invested in Enron stock, but took Hill's advice and sold the company stock. This client and others who acted on the wise advice preserved a significant portion of their 401(k) accounts, and sold at a good price.

In addition Mr. Hill comments, "The reason we advised clients who were Enron employees to sell their Enron stock was strictly from a diversification standpoint. No one should have 80% of their retirement in one stock no matter what company. The client took the initiative to sit down with a CFP® profes-sional, to pay a fee, and to look over all the pieces of their financial life. That's what led to the saving of their 401(k)s."

They Were Pro-Active

This may seem like a pretty simplistic statement, but most of the individuals in this chapter preserved their savings by being pro-active. The people who didn't lose their money in the Enron stock plunge appear to have been individuals who either sought out quality, professional financial advice, or preserved their wealth themselves by applying the basic financial princi-ple of diversification. Both groups have something in common in that they both took action to become informed, and then followed through with actions that protected their money. It's reassuring to know that if you simply are pro-active on very basic financial principles that you can, in most cases, protect your money.

They Took the Advice of Knowledgeable Financial Advisors

Throughout this chapter you have seen examples of how Enron employees turned to competent financial advisors for assistance. Later in the book, I'll show you how to sort out the advisors that are wolves in sheep's clothing from the ones that are gold.

4   CHOICES MADE
LOSSES WORSE

et's look at what happened to the Enron employees and learn from what happened to them so their pain and anguish won't be in vain.

It's important to understand what Enron employees mean when they state in media interviews how much they lost. They usually are referring to the amount they had in August of 2000. If you've ever seen an area after a river has flooded, you can see a high water mark where the flood crested. August of 2000 was the flood crest for the Enron stock price. The flood dissipated a little after August, then surged again, hitting a second crest in December of 2000, and then slowly ebbed away until there was a dry gulch at the end of 2001.

If you look at the Enron stock price "flood" in the table on the next page, you can see when the flood crested and then receded. The December 31, 2000 date is highlighted since that is the approximate date used in one of the lawsuits to state the losses.

Sometimes the amount an Enron employee states he or she lost is actually a compilation of amounts in several Enron retirement or compensation plans. The reason this is important

Date	Enron Stock Price
August 17, 2000	$ 90.56
December 31, 2000	$ 83.13
May 9, 2001	$ 59.20
August 15, 2001	$ 40.25
October 29, 2001	$ 13.81
November 13, 2001	$ 9.88
December 7, 2001	$ .75
April 6, 2002	$ .33

is that the Enron 401(k) disaster created great fear among 401(k) participants across America because they thought that something was wrong with 401(k) plans. When you sort through the losses, as they are recorded in the lawsuits, they stem from a wide variety of plans that aren't commonly available to the majority of American employees. The Enron deferred compensation plan is a good example of this. It's estimated the plan had four hundred upper level managers in it out of twenty-one thousand Enron employees. The same pattern is followed at other large corporations with these types of plans. Stock options are another example. Most U.S. companies don't offer stock option plans that reach down to the level of rank and file workers.

Losses stated by the media for specific Enron employees are somewhat lower in certain legal documents filed on their behalf. For one employee it was $300,000 lower and for another $200,000 lower. There are many legitimate reasons for this. The fact the losses are lower than announced in the media, of course, in no way diminishes the trauma these individuals have experienced or lessens any possible Enron responsibility.

In order to understand the next point, let's imagine your 401(k) had $100,000 as of December 31, 1997 and from then until December 31, 2001 it was invested in an S&P 500® index fund. This type of mutual fund approximates the up's and down's of the U.S. stock market and is available in many 401(k) plans. It provides a simple way of showing what the U.S. stock market did during the time period. One of the reasons I chose December 31, 2000 is that it's similar to the date one of the lawsuits uses, and it's easier to compare the losses stated in it.

Let's compare your results to a hypothetical Enron employee, Ima Investor. She has chosen to place 100% of her 401(k) in Enron stock and has $100,000 in her 401(k) on the same date you do, December 31, 1997. Ima leaves 100% of her 401(k) in Enron stock until December 31, 2001. Look at the table on the next page to see how your results compare.

I have highlighted the total reached by the period ending December 31, 2000, so that you can see the vast difference be-

51

Year	You	S&P 500®	Ima Investor	Enron Stock
Amount at start: Dec. 31, 1997	$100,000		$100,000	
As of: Dec. 31, 1998	$127,000	27% +	$140,000	40% +
As of: Dec. 31, 1999	$152,400	20% +	$221,200	58% +
As of: Dec. 31, 2000	$137,160	10% -	**$418,068**	89%+
As of: Dec. 31, 2001	$120,701	12% -	$ 4,097	98% -

(A) Factors such as 401(k) fees or growth due to the addition of company match haven't been included.

(B) All figures rounded off.

tween what you would have received as a return in your 401(k) if you had the same return as the U.S. stock market (what the S&P 500® reflects), and what Ima Investor would have received by having 100% of her 401(k) in Enron stock. As you can see Ima Investor has dramatically more.

It's important to note, the sky-high price of Enron stock that allowed the growth of Ima Investor's 401(k) was pumped up by what appear to be utter falsehoods created by elaborate accounting tricks. If a company can keep its stock price growing by leaps and bounds far ahead of the U.S. stock market average, investors flock to buy the stock, which can allow the company access to more money to fuel the growth of the company. It also permits the company's executives to cash out of their vast amounts of company stock at lucrative prices.

Despite the Enron stock price being pumped up, if Ima Investor had sold her Enron stock as of December 31, 2000, she would have received $418,068 to invest elsewhere in the Enron 401(k). She could have sold her inflated company stock at any point prior to the problems with the "lockdown" and retained a significant portion.

Now, let's look at the amount you would have had on December 31, 2000. Your amount would have been $137,160. This amount represents the growth or loss in the U.S. stock market during the time period we are using. Ima Investor, by being totally invested in Enron stock, would have earned $280,908 more than you by December 31, 2000. That is a lot more!

Now look at the amount your 401(k) lost in the year 2000. It lost 10%. The U.S. stock market was doin' realllly lousy in the year 2000, so the Enron stock going up and up and up looked like a sure-fire winner to Enron employees. Going up

89% in one year is phenomenal, especially when the rest of the U.S. stock market is in the tank. So, now you see why so many Enron employees threw 100% of their 401(k)s into Enron stock.

In 2001 when Lockheed Martin stock was going up and the rest of the U.S. stock market was heading south, we frequently heard its employees say, "I put all my 401(k) in Lockheed Martin stock – it's the only thing going up." This is very common for 401(k) participants to do. Remember, however, what goes up, often will come down.

Individual Cases of Losses

A s we look at what specific Enron employees lost, I don't want to cause further pain to individuals, so I won't use their names. I'll refer to them as "Enron Employee #1," and "Enron Employee #2."

Enron Employee #1

His stated loss is $66,000. At one time, he was a participant in the ESOP, but wisely moved his money into the 401(k) because no loss is listed for it. Some of his loss is attributable to the pension plan, but it's unclear how much. The rest is from choosing to keep his money in Enron Stock in the 401(k). Since he was able to remove all of his money from the ESOP, it's safe to assume he was over age 50 and had the right to transfer his company match out of Enron stock.

Let's assume for a moment the entire loss was in his 401(k). How much would he have contributed to end up with $66,000? How much does that compare to your imaginary 401(k) growing at the same rate as the U.S. stock market? We'll again use an S&P 500® index fund to help us estimate the growth of your imaginary 401(k).

As you can see from the table on the next page, Enron Employee #1 contributed approximately $15,788, but ended up in three years with $66,005. If you had put $15,788 in your imaginary 401(k) in an S&P 500® index fund, then you would have ended up with only $21,655. That is a $44,350 difference!

Enron Employee #2

This person is one of two individuals who have the highest stated amounts lost. In stories in the media, this individual was said to have lost $1.3 million. In the lawsuit he is participating in, his loss is stated as $1 million. (Again, there can be legitimate reasons for this difference.)

This Enron employee chose to hold approximately 83% of his money in the Enron ESOP, which only held Enron stock, and 17% in Enron stock in the Enron 401(k). He has stated he chose to keep 100% of his retirement money in Enron stock. This implies he elected to have his employee contribution go into the Enron Corporation Stock Fund and chose not to diversify it into any of the other investments available. The company

Year	You	S&P 500®	Enron Employee #1	Enron Stock
Amount at start: **Dec. 31, 1997**	$15,788		$15,788	
As of: **Dec. 31, 1998**	$20,051	27% +	$22,103	40% +
As of: **Dec. 31, 1999**	$24,061	20% +	$34,924	58% +
As of: **Dec. 31, 2000**	**$21,655**	10% -	**$66,005**	89%+
As of: **Dec. 31, 2001**	$19,056	12% -	$ 1,320	98% -

(A) Factors such as 401(k) fees or growth due to the addition of company match haven't been included.

(B) All figures rounded off.

(C) For the sake of simplicity, we are assuming he didn't take any distributions or loans that would have affected the amount of money in this 401(k).

(D) This person appears to have left Enron employment in 1998 and for the sake of simplicity we haven't calculated any company match being contributed.

match was paid in Enron stock into the Enron Corporation Stock Fund. So the 17% can assumed to be his contributions and the company match.

Since articles about him have stated he retired at age 62 in the year 2000, this means he had the right for many years to sell all his company match and diversify his money into other investments in the 401(k), but had chosen not to do so.

He left his money in an out-of-favor, difficult to manage plan. In 1994, Enron began winding down the ESOP and encouraging employees age 50 and over to move their money out of it using three distribution methods. One of which was to transfer it into the Enron 401(k) where it could be diversified.

It was difficult for employees to get their money out of the ESOP. The money could only be moved in 20% increments per year, so it took five years to move all the money. The requests for the distribution had to be made in writing and arrive at the plan trustee by the 20th of any month. The employee's Enron stock in the ESOP was then sold over the last ten days of the month. The distribution would go into the 401(k) to be invested as the employee directed or would be paid out in one of the other distribution methods. The process was complicated and slow, but nevertheless, many Enron employees made the move so that by January 1, 2001 only about 39% of the assets were still in the plan.

Enron Employee #2 had the right for seven years to move the approximately $1 million he had in the ESOP. I assume he had received notices and instructions over the seven years since a large number of his co-workers who were age 50 or over had moved their money out during that time frame.

It's not uncommon for employees to be passive in their 401(k) plans. Since our firm counsels 401(k) participants, we often receive calls from people needing advice. One of the 401(k)s that we often assist people in was terminating two of its investment options. For almost a year, the plan sent notices to participants informing them these two options would no longer be available by such-and-such a date, and to please move their money into one of the other investment options in the plan. Evidently, few people in the two investments paid attention. The plan extended the deadline, and sent more notices. Still, employees continued to have money in the two investments. Shortly before the final deadline, the plan sent a terse notice informing employees in the two investments their money would be moved into other investments in the plan. Just days before the termination, we received frantic calls from some of the employees in these two investments wanting to know why this was happening and panicked about what they should do. This was after ONE YEAR of information being sent to them.

We appreciate that these employees value our advice, and we assisted them. Still, this is a good example of how many employees in 401(k)s aren't pro-active.

Employee #2 appears to have left his money in the default investments in his plans. Nationally, this is very common.

A significant percentage of 401(k) participants never move out of the default investment for their employee contributions.

A few years ago our firm's senior portfolio manager conducted a private workshop for a small group of employees at a Fortune 500® firm. Their 401(k) plan was making changes, and they needed assistance. In the course of conversation, he discovered the group had been with the company an average of twenty-five years, and none of them had made *any* investment changes in all those years.

Still another example concerns a sharp, intelligent, capable woman who took me completely by surprise when she asked if there were any investment options in her 401(a) plan (similar to 401(k)s but contain only company contributions). For years she had missed that her quarterly 401(a) statements showed other investments were available. She had left the company contributions in the default investment.

In articles about Enron Employee #2, he stated he had chosen to put 100% of his retirement money in Enron stock. Let's look at how much, approximately, he put in his 401(k) compared to your imaginary 401(k). As you can see in the table on the next page, his 401(k) grew almost $500,000 in the year 2000 from the growth in the Enron stock price. That is a stunning amount. I'm sure you and I both would like to see our 401(k)s do that trick!

The sad fact is that he could have sold and preserved his savings.

59

Year	You	S&P 500®	Enron Employee #2	Enron Stock
Amount at start: Dec. 31, 1997	$239,196		$239,196	
As of: Dec. 31, 1998	$303,779	27% +	$334,874	40% +
As of: Dec. 31, 1999	$364,535	20% +	$529,102	58% +
As of: Dec. 31, 2000	$328,081	10% -	$1,000,002	89%+
As of: Dec. 31, 2001	$288,711	12% -	$ 20,000	98% -

(A) Factors such as 401(k) fees or growth due to the addition of company match haven't been included.

(B) All figures rounded off.

(C) For the sake of simplicity, we are assuming he didn't take any distributions or loans that would have affected the amount of money in this 401(k).

(D) This individual retired, and for simplicity we haven't allowed for any company match to be added to these figures.

Final Thoughts About the Losses

A s you can observe from the cases of these two Enron employees, the Enron inflated stock price is what created the
very high values in the Enron 401(k) and also the very high
losses. Of course, no amount of math and hindsight can ease the
pain and hardship from the tremendous losses these individuals
have suffered. The amounts the Enron employees lost, and the
affect on their lives, is truly heartbreaking, and they deserve our
compassion.

It's important to understand that we have wired into us a
desire to feel important and be part of something special. These
desires can make us great employees. We work hard and enjoy
seeing the company be successful. We feel good about contributing and feel a loyalty toward our company. These same tendencies can lead us into trouble when we are making choices in our
401(k)s. We tend to lose perspective and believe loyalty to the
company means owning lots of company stock. We tend to
believe the positive news company executives are saying about
the company. We think we have special knowledge of the company because we work there. Somehow our emotions get all
bound up with company stock, and we lose our perspective. It's
very easy to do.

One of the lessons we can learn from the terrible disaster that happened to the Enron employees is there are powerful,
psychological and behavioral forces at work in each one of us

that must be recognized and controlled in order to make good choices to sell company stock in our individual 401(k) accounts.

A friend of mine was laid off from a technology company whose stock had done well. She confided to me that during her employment with the company she had decided to not diversify her 401(k), but had kept it 100% in company stock. She told me, "It worked out for me, but it could just have easily been like Enron. I am very fortunate."

PART 2

ESSENTIAL

KNOWLEDGE

TO

PROTECT

YOUR

401(K)

5   KEEP YOUR 401(K)

FROM BEING

ENRON'D

There are fundamental truths you can apply to protect your 401(k). I can't guarantee that in every instance your money will be protected, but I will say that if you apply the principles in this chapter you'll greatly increase your odds of protecting your 401(k). Every day thousands of employees in 401(k)s violate these principles and endanger their money. You, however, are doing a very smart thing. You're reading this book.

Smart Things to Avoid

Each of these really zapped the Enron employees. These five items can be like rattlesnakes that slither up to you quietly, and strike when you least expect it. Their venom destroyed millions of hard-earned dollars in the Enron 401(k) and ESOP plans. But Enron employees aren't the only ones who have had these rattlesnakes sidle up to them. These are five, easy errors for any 401(k) participant to make. And many do. These are easy mistakes to make. Too easy. But you're smart, and you're learning.

Don't Rely On What Company Management Says About Company Stock

Enron employees aren't the only employees who have been told a tall tale by their company's management in order to get them to buy company stock. One of our good friends at a Fortune 500® corporation reached the age where he could sell the company stock that was company match in his 401(k) account. It was a large amount of his account, and he wanted to sell it and diversify into other investments. The firm's top management sent out a "dog and pony show" to rally the middle managers to convince the rank and file workers the company stock price would be climbing. His manager told him excitedly about the special information he had just learned about how great the firm was doing, and how the stock price was going to shoot up. Our friend is an intelligent, careful individual, but management wooed him, and he kept his company stock. After watching the stock price fall, he learned some top managers had been selling their stock while touting it as a buy to the troops.

Stories like this make your blood boil, and shows how easily even the most careful among us can be wooed. Now with the Internet, it's easy to find out if your company's upper management is telling you one thing, and voting with their pocketbooks another. By law, certain members of upper management must report when they buy and sell their personal holdings of the company's stock. This information becomes public record. To see if your top management is buying or selling simply:

1) Go to, http://finance.yahoo.com/quotes?symbols

2) Enter the symbol for your company's stock in the left entry box.

3) In the right entry box, click on "Research" in the pull down menu.

4) Click "Get."

5) In the "More Info" menu bar click "Insiders."

6) Scroll down to see whether management insiders are buying or selling.

Now, this isn't a perfect solution. Insider selling is common even when a company's stock is doing well, but if you pay attention, over time you may see a pattern.

Don't Keep More Than 5% to 12% of Your 401(k) in Company Stock

During the year 2000 the stock market was losing money like crazy, Enron employees saw their company stock going up and piled on. Yes, Enron management appears to have encouraged it, but so did the stock market.

Despite the fact Enron management appears to have strongly recommended Enron employees be heavily invested in company stock, some employees were smarter than their bosses. As I've mentioned before, according to one of the Enron lawsuits, approximately 40% of the Enron 401(k) wasn't in Enron stock, and only 11% of the Enron stock owned by Enron employees in the 401(k) was reportedly due to the company match. It appears some employees were selling off the company match and diversifying into other investments. Smart cookies.

A good rule of thumb, based on statistical evidence, is to not hold more than 5% to 12% of your 401(k) in your company's stock.

Mark Gleason, CFA and Senior Financial Advisor of Wescap Management Group, comments, "Certainly at a minimum, it makes sense to move away from company stock when you're allowed to under the 401(k) plan. Putting both investment capital and 'human capital' (your employment related income potential) in the same firm makes no sense. If a firm has problems, not only does the stock go down, but bonuses decline and salary may be reduced or eliminated (if you're downsized). No matter how good the prospects of the firm are, it always makes strategic sense to diversify away from the company stock."

Many financial advisors find employees are very reluctant to let go of their company stock. Studies have found that employees don't think their company's stock is very risky. This has certainly been the experience of Timothy M. Hayes, President, Landmark Financial Advisory Services, LLC. "I've counseled several clients recently who have a very high percentage of their investments in their company's stock. I have found many are very reluctant to divest the company stock. I saw this same mentality in a client I worked with a year ago who was associated with Ford. He had nearly all of his net worth in company stock. I suggested he divest at least a portion of it, but he chose not to diversify. Subsequently, he suffered a very big loss when Ford company stock dropped dramatically."

Many Enron employees were below the age limit for selling the company stock they received as a company match in their 401(k)s. Many 401(k) participants across America are in similar circumstances. If you're in this situation, don't buy more company stock that would take you over the 5% to 12% limit. As soon as you have an opportunity to sell the company stock that has been restricted, then take it down to the 5% to 12% limit. If you take a job at a new company, then you have the opportunity to move your 401(k) to an IRA or your new employer's 401(k) (if the new plan will accept it). Take advantage of the move, to sell your company stock to be within the recommended percentage limit. If you don't have these options, then put an extra effort into saving outside of your 401(k).

Don't Leave More Than 5% to 12% in Company Stock After Retiring

Violating this principle resulted in some of the saddest Enron stories. It apparently never occurred to the Enron retirees who left their money 100% in Enron stock in the Enron 401(k) or

ESOP what an incredibly dangerous thing they were doing by keeping ALL of their money in ONE stock. This is very, very dangerous. Diversify your investments.

Just in case you think this couldn't happen to you, here is a story about one of the best companies in America. Procter & Gamble (P&G) stock has been well-known for steady growth for many years. Rob Moody, M.S., CFA, CFP®, CLU, ChFC of Compass Advisors, LLC tells of beginning to work with a client in 1999 who had just left P&G after a long career with the company. He describes what happened, "The client's entire 401(k) was in P&G stock and was worth $1.2 million at the time. I recommended he roll it into an IRA and diversify it, which we did for him in early 2000. Over the next few weeks, P&G stock lost over half its value. He is now semi-retired at age 50, and drawing over $7,200 per month from his IRA, which is now worth more than $1.5 million. His former P&G co-workers are still working."

Richard K. Hammel, Senior Advisor and a CFP® professional of Hammel Financial Advisory Group, LLC counseled a couple in which the wife was the primary earner and the husband stayed home. The wife was taking early retirement because the company was closing its office in the area where she lived. The couple's investment portfolio was 95% company stock (a 401(k) and stock options). "To say we were extremely concerned about the situation is putting it mildly. We knew this was a dangerously high percentage for them. The bottom line of the story is that we encouraged them to sell off the majority of the stock, which they did. The sale was completed at a good price shortly before the September 11 attack and the market's decline. We were very thankful to have helped them preserve their retirement portfolio."

Don't Wait to Sell until You Make Your Money Back

There is a powerful behavioral tendency among investors to not sell a stock that has gone down in value because they want to make their money back before selling it. This is a common and well-documented investor behavioral tendency.

The Enron stock price fell from around $90 in August 2000 to around $25 in mid-September 2001, which is before the earliest date I have seen for problems from the "lockdown" of the plan. Employees could have sold at any time and kept the profit they had.

Give up. Cut your losses. Save what you can. Move on to another investment.

Don't Leave Your Money in Difficult to Manage Or Out-of-Favor Plans

As you read earlier, it was difficult for Enron employees to extract their money from the Enron ESOP. Employees who wanted to transfer their money out of the plan could only transfer out 20% per year, and had to submit the requests in

writing to the trustee of the plan by the 20th of any month.
Enron began closing down the Enron ESOP plan over seven
years ago, and employees transferred tens of millions of dollars
out of the ESOP. Only ten months before the Enron 401(k)
disaster, employees had transferred 61% of the Enron ESOP's
assets out of the plan.

Some individuals didn't transfer their money out of the
ESOP. Even if they'd wanted to get their money out when the
Enron stock began having severe difficulties in the fall of 2001,
it appears they could have only removed 20% of their money.
For seven years Enron had allowed individuals age 50 and
older who had five years with the company to move their
money out of the ESOP, but some didn't. It's very tragic what
happened to them. Don't get caught the same way. Be pro-
active. Manage your account and take action.

Smart Things to Do

S ometimes it's easy to feel that you and your 401(k) are at the
mercy of factors you can't control, like stock prices or the
crazy 401(k) regulations. If you haven't reached the age at which
you're allowed to diversify the company stock in your 401(k),
then you may feel concerned about this undiversified portion of
your account. If you're near retirement, you may feel worried
about your 401(k) investment returns. It can be comforting to
know there are things you can control that can make a difference.

Diversify Your Investments in Your 401(k)

F. William McNabb III heads up The Vanguard Group's Institutional Investor Group, which runs its very successful 401(k) program for corporations across the country. McNabb recently stated, "The Enron 401(k) disaster shows how important the fundamental principle of diversification is. It's one of the most basic financial principles of 401(k) success." Diversification simply means reducing the danger of losing your money by dispersing it among different types of investments. Though the principle is simple, the application can be tricky. In the next chapter, I'll give you more information about diversification.

Rebalance Your 401(k) Account

David Wray, president of the Profit Sharing/401(k) Council of America, says that rebalancing is one of the most important principles of investing in a 401(k). He believes 401(k) participants should periodically (at least annually) adjust the amount of each of their investments to keep them in line with their original asset allocation decision. (Asset allocation means the variety of investment categories you've selected.)

Rebalancing will keep you from being over exposed to any one investment in the event it zooms ahead of your other investment choices and performs particularly well. Periodic rebalancing also gives you the added advantage of locking in your gains from a company stock by diversifying the profit into other investments in your 401(k). As a result, company stock price plunges like Enron's will have less impact on your 401(k) account. Knowledgeable financial planners frequently use this technique, but it languishes among 401(k) participants.

Your 401(k) account gets out of balance as the company's match in company stock is paid into it, plus as the company's stock price rises, it further throws your account off kilter. A wise thing to do with company stock that has risen is to sell it systematically, and keep your amount of company stock within the recommended limits of 5% to 12% of your 401(k) account.

Lock in Your Profit

Many employees in 401(k) plans don't understand that when company stock goes up dramatically in value, as the Enron stock did, it's just a paper profit illusion unless you SELL the stock and take the profit. Remember, what goes up can and does come down. Lock in your profit by selling.

A rule of thumb is to sell 25% of company stock that has gone up 50% in value. Take the proceeds from the sale and put it in diversified investments. If it goes up another 50%, sell another 25% of the original investment, and so forth.

Chuck DiFalco, a friend of mine, has what he calls "Chuck's Law." A stock may go up 30% one year and 50% the next, but the third year, he warns, it's likely to bite you back and drop like a rock, the result being that you lose money instead of making it.

Keep Your Address Current with the Company

This is your responsibility. If you don't do this, then you won't receive your 401(k) plan's notices. By law, a company is considered to have discharged their duty when they mail a notice to you at the address you have on file with the company.

You also have to keep up with what is going on at the company so you won't miss the latest news about the 401(k) (in case a notice gets lost in the mail). This is why I recommend not leaving your money in a former employer's 401(k). It's just really, really tough to keep fully informed about your old employer's plan, plus as the years roll on to remember to update your address with an old employer. It's very easy for you to become separated from your old 401(k) money – forever.

In one of the Enron 401(k) participants' lawsuits, some ex-employees assert they weren't notified the Enron 401(k) was going to have a "lockdown." It's very likely a few (I'm not saying all) of these ex-employees didn't keep their addresses up-to-date with their old employer, so the notices didn't arrive at their current address.

A small detail like this seems trivial until – Wham! You see someone lose their retirement money because of it.

I was talking with the head of a major corporation's 401(k) plan who told me every year they have thousands of ESOP dividend checks returned in the mail because participants' addresses are wrong. This is free money, and people still don't change their address with the company!

Seek Advice from a Knowledgeable Financial Advisor

I want to emphasize that it's deeply sad so many hard-working Enron employees lost so much. Out of the ashes of this disaster, however, you have the opportunity to learn valuable lessons. One of these lessons is that many Enron employees didn't seek advice on how to protect their 401(k) money. On the other hand, some did, which resulted in them preserving a substantial portion of their 401(k)s.

If You're in a Special Management Plan, Get Good Advice

An estimated four hundred Enron employees and former employees were in a management deferred compensation plan. The person who was the plan administrator for the Enron deferred compensation plan has stated, through his attorney, that he didn't grant ex-employees' their requests for withdrawals in the last weeks before the bankruptcy, but did grant current employees' requests. Those who weren't able to withdraw their money prior to the bankruptcy, lost everything in these plans. These plans aren't protected in a bankruptcy as 401(k) plans are.

A discussion of these types of plans is far beyond the scope of this book, but if you're in one, seek professional financial advice. These types of compensation plans are very tricky. Not only is company bankruptcy a risk, but taxes are also a concern. Knowledgeable and skilled financial professionals have techniques that can help you.

Be Pro-Active

All of the advice in this chapter simply boils down to being pro-active. Rebalance your investments in your 401(k). Double-check what management tells you about company stock. Keep your address current with the company. Get advice from a caring, competent financial advisor. These things take time, and life is busy. The alternative, however, can be devastating.

Many 401(k) participants have felt the Enron disaster came out of nowhere, and are fearful the same thing will happen to them. The secret of success in your 401(k) is simple. Right actions produce right results. Most employees won't know about confidential comments of auditors, or conversations between top executives that might clue them into knowing whether to sell company stock, or if an accounting disaster is about to occur to the company. The good news is that by being pro-active and doing a few basics, you have a much greater chance of protecting your money.

Some Enron employees were pro-active in their 401(k)s and in the ESOP. One of the 401(k) participants' lawsuits says that just in the year 2000, Enron employees sold $56 million dollars of company stock in the Enron ESOP and moved their money into the Enron 401(k) where they could select diversified investments. Almost 40% of the Enron 401(k) was not invested in company stock. Apparently, some Enron employees were applying the principle of diversification.

Enron employees have had to endure great difficulty, but if you learn from their difficulties to be pro-active, then to a certain extent, their anguish hasn't have been in vain.

6 KNOW YOUR 401(K)
SO YOU CAN
PROTECT IT

Understanding how your 401(k) works can give you insights into how to protect it. One of the top attorneys in the country on distributions from qualified plans (the family of plans 401(k)s are in) has stated this is one of the most complex areas of federal regulations. So, if you feel confused about your 401(k), you're not alone; a lot of professionals feel the same way! In this chapter I'll try to shed some light on 401(k)s so you can understand better how to protect your money. The last chapter of this book will have the action items in this chapter in an easy-to-use checkoff list.

Prior to the mid-1970's, employees didn't have many of the rights and protections they do now in their retirement plans. In the mid-1970's federal legislation was passed that is referred to as ERISA. This legislation changed retirement plans in a dramatic way, and gave participants far more rights.

One day, not long after ERISA passed, a fellow named Ted Benna was studying the Internal Revenue Code, Section

401, paragraph (k), and realized it might be possible to create a special type of retirement plan. WAP! 401(k)s were born.

At that time, employers who had pension plans were tired of being dragged into court by employees who thought the pension plans were being poorly invested. Employees wanted more investment control of their retirement plans. What should come down the pike, but a type of retirement plan that put the investment responsibilities on the employee-participants. This is great, thought employers and employees. Over the next two decades employers began offering 401(k)s, and pension programs began to decline. Today there are around fifty million participants in 401(k)s and other profit sharing plans. Employees have embraced 401(k)s because it gives them a chance to have more money for retirement by investing in the stock market. Enron reminds us, "Be careful what you wish for."

After public disasters like Enron, it's easy to forget the over two decades of 401(k) success. David Wray of the Profit Sharing/401(k) Council of America recently pointed out that one of the reasons Enron or other 401(k) implosions make such startling news is because they are so rare. Since they are emblazoned in peoples memories, people think they have happened frequently. In reality, Enron-style 401(k) disasters are the exception, not the rule.

Millions of people have benefited from 401(k) participation: retirees have retired to good retirements; new homeowners have used 401(k) loans for the purchase; and, children have had college paid for out of their parents 401(k) savings. To take advantage, however, of the numerous benefits of your 401(k), and to protect your money, there are things you *must* know.

Essential 401(k) Knowledge

I t's easy in a 401(k) to feel overwhelmed by all the rules, all the bureaucracy, and all the investment responsibilities. If you understand some essentials, then you can feel less over-whelmed. You can be in charge and take the right steps to keep your money safe. Here is a look at the key parts of a 401(k).

The Plan Sponsor

The plan sponsor is the owner of plan. Usually, it will be your employer. The plan sponsor hires the important companies or personnel who run the plan. In addition, the sponsor creates the plan. Enron was the sponsor of it's 401(k) plan.

The Plan Administrator

The plan administrator is the manager of the plan and has re-sponsibility for the day-to-day operations. Typically, the admin-istrator is in your company's finance or benefits department. The Enron plan administration committee hired a new 401(k) trustee and the transition resulted in the "lockdown."

The Plan Custodian

The plan custodian keeps track of all the money in the 401(k) and keeps it safe. Larger custodians usually have representatives available by telephone to answer your questions about the plan. More and more are offering Web-based services. Many 401(k) participants think bells and whistles, like Web-based services, are fantastic. Keep in mind, however, that you're paying for the services the custodian provides. Those payments come right out of your 401(k) (some plans vary).

The plan custodian can also be referred to as the plan trustee. The new Enron trustee after the "lockdown" is Hewitt.

Your Plan's Information System

Your plan may have a telephone system or a Web site to use to do tasks for your 401(k) account. These information systems are often mysteries to 401(k) participants. I find many participants don't know the customer service telephone number, or don't know how to access the Web site.

Find out what your plan's customer service telephone number is, then call to obtain any information available on the telephone system or the Web site for your plan. Some telephone-based plan information systems have brochures that take you step-by-step through the maze of telephone options. Some Web sites have excellent tools for understanding your 401(k) and keeping your money safe.

Some plan custodians have extras. The Vanguard Group is an excellent example. This custodian has collaborative browsing, which enables a Vanguard representative to chat with you on the telephone while taking "control" of your Web browser and giving you a guided tour of the Vanguard Web site (www.Vanguard.com). It also has "Participant Experience," a brand-new, state-of-the-art Web site for retirement plan participants.

Your plan's information system probably offers more than a way to complete transactions for your account. It probably gives you access to customer service representatives who can answer questions about your plan. Call for information when your perplexed about the plan.

Here is a warning: In recent court cases, plan representatives haven't been held responsible for giving plan participants inaccurate information. This applies to your plan custodian's customer service representatives, your company's human resource representatives, your manager, or just about anyone else in your company or associated with the plan custodian. Courts have ruled that the SPD and plan document are the authoritative source, NOT what any company or plan representative tells you about the plan.

As appalling as that is, you might be able to secure some assistance in your company's or the plan custodian's bureaucracy if you can rattle off the name of the representative who gave you the inaccurate information. This is especially important if it was a plan custodian's representative because there is strong competition between custodians to nab companies' retirement plans as clients. Due to this competition, your plan custodian may be very responsive to helping solve your problem before your company finds one of the custodian's employees has fouled up.

Here is a tip: If at all possible, get the FULL name of the representative you speak with and jot down the date and time. You will need the full name because some plan custodians have call centers in several areas of the country that rotate picking up incoming calls. Telling a supervisor that you spoke with Cheryl on March 23 may not help if there is one Cheryl in each of the three call centers. It's also very important to have the date AND the time you called, because most plan custodians record incoming calls. By giving the date and time, a supervisor can request the correct recording and listen to the conversation.

The Plan Document

The plan document is a thick, legal document, usually custom-designed for a large employer by their own group of attorneys. (Typically, smaller businesses use generic plans supplied by the 401(k) custodian, such as Fidelity or Vanguard.) The plan document states how the company's 401(k) plan will be run. The people who run the plan are required to operate it according to the rules the plan document states. Some 401(k) plans allow things that others don't. For instance, a minority of plans allow participants to remove all their money from the plan while they are still working for the employer who sponsors the plan (called an in-service distribution). Most plans don't allow this. Most 401(k) plans allow participants to remove their money when they leave the company at any age. Some won't allow you to have it until age 65.

The Summary Plan Description

The plan document is so complicated, that some of them can leave even pros scratching their heads as to exactly what the creators meant. Fortunately, the law requires your plan to supply you with a summary of the plan document, called a Summary Plan Description (SPD). Some of these are actually fun to read; others are real yawners. All the basics of your plan are in there (or should be): what your rights are; where your contributions go; how you can get distributions; details about getting loans; and, so forth.

Reading the SPD is very important for you to know how to protect your money. You should have received an SPD when you began participating in your 401(k) plan; but if your copy has wandered away to parts unknown, or if you've had your SPD for a long time and it might be outdated, then call the customer service number for your 401(k) plan and order another one.

If you work for a large corporation that has bought other companies, then there is probably more than one 401(k) plan in use in your corporation. Each of the companies the corporation purchases often has its own 401(k) plan. Sometimes these plans are continued, and sometimes they are merged into the primary 401(k) plan for the corporation. A huge corporation I counsel employees in, has approximately twenty, distinct 401(k) plans each with separate SPDs and different rules. The customer service representatives for the custodian who services them sometimes becomes confused and sends out the wrong plan's SPD. In fact, one time an entire division of the corporation was sent SPDs for the wrong plan.

It's important you have the correct SPD for your plan, so you can make good decisions. Giving the customer service representative the formal name of your plan when you call to order the SPD will help you receive the correct one. Usually the formal name of your 401(k) plan appears at the top of your 401(k) account statement. When the SPD comes, double-check again that it's the proper one for your plan. The plan's official name is usually on the cover. If not, check toward the back of the SPD where legal statements can usually be found about your rights. The formal name of the plan should be stated there.

Sometimes your employer or plan custodian goofs up and creates a booklet that doesn't meet the technical requirements for it to be an SPD. Though this might seem like a fine point of law to some, it can and does happen. One plan I've studied extensively, and have notebooks full of historical documents on, doesn't have a true SPD as it's most recent booklet summarizing the plan. When participants in the plan call in and request an SPD for the plan, they are sent this non-SPD booklet. The customer service representatives refer to it on the telephone as an SPD, but it's not an SPD. It's missing important legal documentation and protection tips. You don't have to be a 401(k) specialist to do a basic double-check of the SPD your company sends you. Simply read the booklet. Sometimes there will be a legal statement in the front of the booklet, or in the first few paragraphs of the booklet, that state it's an SPD. If you don't see it there, then flip to the back of the booklet. If you see statements stating your ERISA rights as a plan participant, who the plan sponsor is, and other legal details, then in all probability, it's a true SPD.

Thirdly, sometimes the SPD for your 401(k) plan isn't an accurate representation of what the plan document actually says. This happens far more than you would think it would. If you're faithfully following the rules in the SPD, and it's not accurate, you may be missing valuable benefits or even endangering your money. The only way to know if the SPD is accurate is to order the plan document and check the SPD against it. At first, this may seem like a daunting task, which it can be. But if you focus on the important items to review, you can do it. Look in the back of your SPD in the legal statements about the plan. The SPD should state how you can order the plan document. (In Appendix A, "Ordering Your 401(k) Plan's Information," I have a sample letter for you to use.)

Once you receive this imposing document, sit down in a quiet place for a review of the significant sections of the plan. The most important parts of the plan document for you to compare with the SPD are the rules about contributions, and the rules about distributions. There should be a table of contents at the beginning of the plan stating where these sections can be found in the document. Simply put the plan document and the SPD side by side and look to see if any significant details in these sections are different or missing in either document.

Don't worry about understanding it all. You won't. Just look for the big picture items. For instance, one of the 401(k) plans I frequently counsel participants about is missing an important distribution method from the SPD. The custodian of the plan knows it's available, and employees can use the method (if somehow they know about it), but there isn't a word of it in the SPD. If I hadn't reviewed the plan document, I wouldn't have known this distribution method was available. It wasn't lost in the details of the plan document. The document clearly stated three distribution methods and the SPD stated two.

Now here's a catch: What if you compare your SPD with your plan document, and your SPD has an *additional* benefit not contained in the plan document? Originally, the plan document was considered the legal, governing document for the plan, but recent court cases have forced companies to honor additional benefits stated in their SPDs. If you discover this, and it's a significant benefit, proceed carefully, you may need to seek legal advice as to whether you can take advantage of the additional benefit. (If you decide to get a legal opinion, you should call your state bar association and ask for the names of the ERISA attorneys in your area of the state.)

For your protection, the SPD for your 401(k) plan is required to be updated after a certain number of years. Sometimes, however, your employer changes your plan in between the SPD updates or simply doesn't update it. That is why the next item is so important.

The Summary of Material Modifications

When your employer changes the rules of how your 401(k) plan works, then all plan participants must be notified. The notice of the change, which includes a description of the change, is called a Summary of Material Modifications (SMM). These notices can announce a variety of changes including a reduction of your benefits or an opportunity you need to take advantage of in order to protect your 401(k).

These notices are very important. When you order your plan document, you should also order the SMMs for your plan. Usually these sheets are written in legalese, but they are still very valuable. Once I was reviewing one that went on at length in small type in lots of dense, legal language. I just happened to

notice a small, casual reference to a change in one of the investment funds in the plan at the very end of the document. If I
hadn't persevered in reading the entire document, I wouldn't
have learned that one of the conservative bond funds in the
401(k) had been modified to include a risky, new element. I was
able to alert some of the participants and help them make a
better, safer choice.

File these important documents with your SPD and
plan announcements.

Plan Announcements

Many 401(k) participants leave these unopened. Probably a lot
of Enron employees, and former employees with their money
still in the Enron 401(k), did the exact same thing with the
announcement about the plan "lockdown." Make sure you read
them.

I received a call recently from a 401(k) participant who
asked if I knew such-and-such about a certain investment in her
401(k) plan. It was clear from her question, she didn't know
almost all of the investments in her 401(k) plan had been
changed *a year and a half ago*. She hadn't opened and read the
plan announcements of the changes the plan sent her prior to
the switch. She hadn't opened and read notices informing her if
she didn't change her old investment options they would be
automatically changed to certain new ones. She hadn't opened

and read the large package sent to her by the plan listing all the new investment options. She hadn't opened or read the announcements about, or even known, her plan was "locked down" for a month (just like the Enron plan) while the new investments were put in place. Not only had she missed all these things, but she'd received her 401(k) account statements every three months for a year and a half, and hadn't noticed the investments had changed or worse – possibly hadn't even read any of her account statements during that time. Unfortunately, many 401(k) participants do the same thing.

IRS 5500 Forms

Your plan must file an IRS 5500 form for each plan year. It states various details like number of participants, the plan administrator's telephone number, where the 401(k)'s money is kept, total assets in the plan, plan expenses, the yearly independent auditor's report, and other interesting facts. You can order it when you order the plan document. Unfortunately, the most current IRS 5500 form available, due to various regulations, is usually for two years ago, but it still is very useful.

Your Pay Stub

One of your most important 401(k) documents is your pay stub. It usually shows if your contribution is going into your 401(k). Employers make mistakes. Accounting glitches occur. Sometimes your money is left in your paycheck and doesn't go into your account. It can be a nightmare to get the mistake reversed.

A participant who had this happen called and called until he finally located a person in his company who could possibly help him. She told him this type of error occurred frequently due to a glitch in the payroll computer system.

Investment Instruction Receipts

After moving your money from one investment to another within your 401(k), double-check to make sure the investment transaction was executed. If you have a telephone-based information system, call in a couple of days (or the appropriate period for your plan) to make sure your instructions were followed. If you have a Web-based system, check your account there.

You're usually sent an investment instruction receipt confirming the change. Make sure when the receipt arrives that it accurately states the investment change you requested. When your 401(k) account statement arrives, use the receipt to double-check the statement. If something doesn't look right, call the customer service number for your 401(k) plan. Don't let problems slide. Protect your money by acting promptly.

Your 401[k] Account Statement

It's important to read your 401(k) account statement every time it comes. When you receive the statement, double-check to make sure everything is correct. Did the custodian make the investment change? Was your 401(k) loan payment credited to your account? Don't let anything slip through the cracks.

Your Plan's Beneficiary Forms

These forms are extremely important, but there are two problems with them that can easily trip you up.

The first is that either your employer or the plan custodian might misplace your beneficiary forms. Once your form is lost, as far as the system is concerned, you never had one. There is no proof that you ever filed it, unless your beneficiary can produce a signed and dated copy showing it was received by your company or the plan custodian.

A good thing to do is to send the filled-out, signed, original beneficiary form and a copy of the filled-out, signed, beneficiary form to the custodian of the 401(k) (your plan may require a different location), along with a self-addressed envelope, and a letter requesting a representative sign the copy and date it with the date received, then mail it back to you. The key to this system working is to file the copy returned to you in a safe place, preferably with your will. It's also a good idea to make a copy of the filled-out and signed beneficiary form, and place it with your other 401(k) information.

Secondly, some 401(k) plans require multiple beneficiary forms. Carefully read the section of your SPD describing what happens to the account at your death. You may find that

93

the SPD mentions more than one pot of money, each requiring a beneficiary form. To obtain more forms, call your plan's customer service number or print them from the plan's Web site.

I know of a company's savings plan that the participants refer to as the "company's 401(k) plan." In reality, it's three separate plans: a 401(k) account, an ESOP account, and a money purchase pension plan. Most participants of this savings plan assume it's one plan because they receive one account statement, and the plan is referred to by one name. Each of the three plans requires a separate beneficiary form to be filed to insure the money in each reaches the correct beneficiary.

In the next chapter, I'll let you know some of the special difficulties with designating your 401(k) account's beneficiaries.

Your Plan's Investments

As I mentioned earlier, diversification simply means reducing the danger of losing your money by dispersing it among different types of investments. It's one of the most important techniques to protect your 401(k) money, but it can be tricky.

Some 401(k) participants think diversification means buying a little bit of everything in their 401(k) plan – sort of just spreading their money around. This can get you in a lot of trouble if you're not careful because not all 401(k)s offer a good, broad mix of investment categories. Sometimes a few of the investment options are essentially copycats of one another. You have to read the literature on the investments in your 401(k) carefully to try and figure out what you're actually being offered. Some 401(k) plans only have information in the Summary Plan Description about the investments. Some 401(k) plans, however, offer more. Call or write the customer service center for your plan, and ask if additional investment information is available.

Let me give you an example that can help you understand this complicated area. One of the 401(k) plans I know well, at one time offered seven different stock mutual funds and four company stock funds (some were stocks of former companies the corporation had purchased). This gave a total of eleven choices. You would think diversification should be pretty easy, right? Well, the truth was, five of the stock mutual funds were copycats of one another since all five were based on the S&P 500® index. Some of the company stock funds and one of the stock mutual funds fell into a second stock category, Value stocks. One teetered on the edge of the Growth category that the S&P 500® funds were under, and the remaining lone investment was a lousy option in the small stock category (it lost 70% in one year).

For diversification purposes, participants really only had two categories to choose from: "Large Growth" represented by the S&P 500® index funds and "Medium Value." Employees thought they were diversifying by buying several funds, but in reality they had only bought one type of fund or maybe two. Their 401(k) accounts weren't widely diversified.

Another thing to understand about diversification is that it tends to cut your losses, but it also tends to cut your profits. Sometimes, however, you have to make the decision to be disciplined and stick with a well-proven principle. For instance, you study the investments in your 401(k) plan, receive advice from a knowledgeable financial advisor, sell some of your company stock, diversify your 40(k) money into several investments, and sit back and watch your company's stock price shoot up just after you sold it. This can drive you crazy.

In such a time as that, here's a good story to keep in mind. A financial advisor with a large national firm had a client in his 40's who had a significant percentage of his net worth in Enron stock. The advisor explained, "I recommended he sell most of the Enron stock. He was only willing to sell one-third. I put the proceeds from the sale of the Enron stock in an investment that gave him diversification, but didn't appreciate as much as the Enron stock at the time. For a while, it looked pretty embarrassing, but you know the outcome. The Enron stock plunged to almost nothing. The diversified portfolio kept its value. Diversification is a word that is sometimes over used, but it means exactly what it says – have your money in diverse investment categories."

The secret to diversifying is first to understand which category the investments in your 401(k) fit into, next select investments that aren't copycats of one another, and then be patient (this last one can be the hardest of all).

This subject is simply too vast and complicated to do justice to here. Check Appendix C for some excellent, investment oriented 401(k) books. Also, to help you select diversified investments in your 401(k), I've provided you with a stock matrix and a bond matrix in Appendix B to help you understand the broad categories into which the investments in your 401(k) fall. Follow the instructions for working with them, and you'll understand more about what true diversification is in your particular 401(k).

Sometimes, it's best to get help from someone who devotes their professional time to the study of the subject and pay to access their expertise. Later in the book, I'll show you how to find a specialist to help you select investment funds in your 401(k).

It's great to know about diversification, but it's useless if you don't know how to move your money between investment funds within the plan. I've found most participants are unsure of how to do this. Some have tried, only to find the process so confusing, they failed and quit trying. If this has been your experience, don't give up. Call the plan's customer service center and ask to be walked through the procedure. Some representatives are more responsive than others, call back and get another one if the first isn't helpful. Stick with it. You must learn how to move your money so you can protect it.

Another very important piece of information for you to know is when you can sell your company stock. I find most of the 401(k) participants I talk to have no idea what the rules are. These people are sitting ducks for an Enron-style company stock plunge. Learn your plan's rules and keep an eye out for the new rules as they come down the pike. This is an area where the law and plan rules may be changing. Your plan's SPD will give you the information that has been valid in the past, but may not be what is valid now or in the near future. Read the SMMs for your plan. If the rules for your plan have been changed, then the change should be in one of these. (If the rule change has been very recent, there may not have been time yet for an SMM to have been created.) Also, call the customer service number for your plan and ask what the current rules are for selling the employer contribution company stock in your account.

Some 401(k) plans have a potentially dangerous investment option sometimes referred to as a "self-managed" option. It allows participants to buy and sell investments offered outside of the 401(k). You usually don't pay a fee to buy or sell investments offered within your 401(k), but through the self-managed option you pay fees (sometimes significant fees) to buy and sell investments. Fees lower your investment returns, but this isn't the only problem.

I was talking with the head of the 401(k) plans for a large corporation, and he admitted the self-managed option that had recently been made available to participants was something that could destroy participants' savings if misused.

How? By allowing participants to buy risky investments through their 401(k)s with the self-managed option. A participant can buy and lose all too quickly in the stock market.

Let me say this clearly, DON'T USE THE SELF-MANAGED OPTION IN YOUR 401(K) UNLESS YOU'RE A VERY EXPERIENCED AND SUCCESSFUL INVESTOR! Less experienced investors are better off using the screened mutual fund choices available within the 401(k) plan.

Your Company's ESOP Plan

Like a 401(k), an ESOP belongs to the category of defined contribution plans. However, an ESOP is different in that it's almost invariably funded by the company, not by employee contributions, and it's invested primarily in company stock. Scott Rodrick, Director of Publishing and Information Technology for the National Center for Employee Ownership explains, "A typical employee ESOP is an extra benefit that is just given to employees, typically in private companies. Only 5% of all ESOPs are in public companies." (Public companies' stock is sold to the public, as opposed to private companies, whose stock isn't offered to the public.)

Some large corporations that are public companies have both a 401(k) and an ESOP. This combination is known as a KSOP. Most participants in a KSOP probably think the ESOP portion is merely an investment fund within the 401(k) plan.

They don't realize an ESOP is a separate plan with separate rules.

As Rodrick mentioned, the company payment into the ESOP is a nice extra for employees. It's easy to think that this company match is your absolute right, but it's good to keep in mind that it's not. For instance, Ford recently stopped its company match, and if some of the more aggressive 401(k) legislation had gone through after the Enron disaster, probably many companies would have dropped their company match.

The important thing to know in order to protect your money in the ESOP, is to know when you have the right to sell the company stock and move it into the 401(k) plan and diversify it. When you move your money into a more diversified position, you increase its safety.

Company Bankruptcy

A 401(k) plan is separate from the company which sponsors it. The money in a 401(k) plan that belongs to the participants isn't company property. Since this is true, then a company bankruptcy doesn't take away the money in the participants' accounts.

Enron's bankruptcy didn't result in money being taken out of the participants' accounts, but it did result in the company stock in those accounts plunging to a fraction of its previous worth. The Enron deferred compensation plan and some other plans were unprotected from bankruptcy.

Essential Protection Information

N ow that you have some essential 401(k) knowledge, let's look at important information to know about protecting your money.

The Greatest Dangers to Your 401(k)

For a moment let's set aside Enron, and look at what the top dangers are to most people's 401(k)s:

Not participating at all or only partially participating so that you don't get your full benefits (such as the full company match). A woman near retirement who was being laid off from her employer was so distressed when she learned from her employer how small her retirement benefits would be that she began throwing up blood at work and went home ill. When I reviewed her retirement plans with her, it was very evident she hadn't paid close attention to them or fully participated during her twenty-five years of employment. Although I managed to help her salvage some extra benefits she didn't know were due to her and would have lost, her total picture was very sad.

Unfortunately, it's not uncommon for employees to not fully participate, then reach retirement and be appalled at how little they will receive in retirement benefits. I was told about a man at a small aerospace company who was eagerly looking forward to his retirement. He hadn't paid attention to his retirement benefits and when he finally figured out how much he would have to live on, he panicked. The co-worker who told me the story said the man claimed the company hadn't kept him informed, but the co-worker said the company had made information available and that he, as well as others, had taken advantage of the information. The co-worker said the man became so distressed, that he had a heart-attack and died.

Don't let these sad stories be repeated in your life. Read your SPD and take the actions needed to get all your company retirement benefits. One of the easiest ways is to contribute enough to receive all the company match.

Not paying attention. Are your contributions going into the plan? Were your investment instructions carried out? Do you know the basic rules of your 401(k) plan? Pay attention and reap the benefits.

Not diversifying.

401(k) Loans. This 401(k) "benefit" is an insidious destroyer of 401(k)s. Never take out a 401(k) loan unless you have to. Never ever use a 401(k) loan to pay for a house. The interest rates are usually higher than financial institutions, the associated fees in many cases are high, and you actually end up paying back *double* what you originally took out.

Listening to co-workers who "know" the plan. Oops! They turn out to be in a different 401(k) with different rules. Oops! They didn't know what they were talking about. Oops! They were passing on bad information from someone else.

I once met with a 401(k) participant who was a supervisor in a small division of a company that was mostly populated by workers acquired from a merger. Human resources at this large corporation would field few questions about the retirement plans. The supervisor told me that employees (including himself) would stand around the hallways talking and talking about their company plan. Everyone was guessing at this and that about the plan. Everyone had an opinion of what the benefits of the plan were. He left me with the impression that this went on frequently and had been going on month after month after month. For some reason, it never occurred to any of them to call the customer service telephone number for the plan and order the information they needed. They just kept wandering around month after month, gossiping from office to office, guessing about their plan.

Read your SPD and learn the correct information about your plan.

Cashing out of the plan when you leave the company. Nationally, this is the number one thing that wipes out 401(k)s. Employees leave the company, and ask for a check, then spend the money. This costs them a large amount in taxes and a 10% early withdrawal penalty if they are under age 59½. Instead, move your money into an IRA or your new employer's 401(k).

Leaving your 401(k) with your former employer. No. No. No. Please don't. This is the way to lose track of your money. Move your money to an IRA or to your next employer.

Create an Open Filing System for Your 401(k) Information

Some people prefer putting information in notebooks, but I've found most people do better with an organized stuffing system. If you have folders already labeled in a file box or filing rack that is convenient to get to, then it's easy to walk by with your newest 401(k) mail and stuff it in the right folder. Quick. Easy. Organized. Here are the folders I suggest you set up:

1) **Pay Stubs:** These are critical to save in case you discover an error, or need to go back and check that you were paid all you were due based on your salary.

2) **The SPD:** Put the SPD, SMMs, and plan announcements in this folder.

3) **401(k) Plan Document.**

4) **Plan Correspondence:** Any correspondence you've exchanged with the plan or company representatives about your 401(k) account should go in this file. Your correspondence can help your financial advisor or ERISA attorney get to the bottom of a problem.

5) **401(k) Account Statements.**

6) **Work History:** It's wise to write down your work history and any retirement plans you were in. I frequently talk with participants that have forgotten an obscure retirement plan at their company which was closed down long ago, but still contains money for them when they retire.

Last fall, I tried to assist a corporate executive with his retirement plans. I explained to him that he had money due to him from a special management plan the company had set aside for him long ago. He stubbornly insisted he had no other money due from any other company retirement plans. I knew better and even brought into the disagreement a well-known, former human resources employee at the company who is a respected specialist in her former company's plans. She told him the money I stated was available and was his to take. He didn't believe me, and I don't think he ever got his money. (The company never let him know it was owed to him at any time during his retirement process. This, unfortunately, is common.)

Another item to include in your work history list is any leave of absences such as maternity leave, or times when you worked for another company.

7) 401(k) Customer Service: Put the customer service telephone number in here along with any information that will help you use the plan's information system better. If you have a PIN number, or other kind of plan identification number, then it should go in here also. This is where you can scribble down the names of the customer representatives who help you.

8) 401(k) Safety Checklist: Photocopy the safety list in the last chapter of this book (you may only photocopy it for your own needs) or place the whole book in the folder. Check off the items as you get them done.

9) Miscellaneous 401(k) Info.

If you're careful and pay attention to what is going on with your 401(k) plan, you'll increase your chances tremendously of protecting your money and achieving 401(k) success.

7   SECRETS ABOUT

BEING IN

A 401(K)

There are many "secrets" about having
your money in a 401(k). Part of my passion is to get
the word out about some of these quirks, so more
participants are aware of the choices they need to
make to protect their money.

Planning for Your Loved Ones

P rotecting your 401(k) money while you're alive is hard
enough, but trying to pass it safely on to your beneficiaries
can be a perplexing problem.

Get Advice About Naming Your Beneficiaries

Make sure you fill the beneficiary forms for your 401(k) out
carefully and correctly. If you've developed a working relationship with a knowledgeable financial advisor, discuss your
beneficiary choices. Beneficiary laws for 401(k)s are complicated. It's easy to make an error and not know it.

Bring your plan's SPD, a list of your beneficiaries, and your plan's beneficiary form to the meeting with your financial advisor. The list of beneficiaries should have the names, ages, social security numbers (if the beneficiary form requires these) and their relationship to you such as: sister, my child, parent, etc. Be prepared to answer questions your advisor may ask you about your goals and what you are trying to accomplish with your beneficiary designations.

Non-Spouse Beneficiary Tax Problems

401(k)s can cause big headaches, and even bigger tax problems, for non-spouse beneficiaries, such as your sister, brother, parents, children, friend, and so forth.

If your spouse inherits your 401(k), she or he can defer paying taxes on the amount by moving your 401(k) money to an IRA in your name, an IRA in his or her name, and into his or her own 401(k).

Beneficiaries who aren't your spouse don't have those tax deferral options. That means the 401(k) money they inherit has to be paid to them and taxed as ordinary income. A small percentage of 401(k) plans allow the distributions to be stretched out over many years, producing a relatively minor tax bill in any given year. Some 401(k) plans allow non-spouse beneficiaries to take the money out over a five-year period, again, reducing the tax bite for any given year. Most 401(k) plans, however, just cut the check and send the money to the

beneficiary. Bam! Boy, oh, boy, does that non-spouse beneficiary have a tax bill! Consequently, an astounding portion of a
401(k) can be lost to taxes. This is especially tragic when a
single parent made her child the primary beneficiary of her
account and was depending on the account to support the
child.

Your Will Doesn't Designate 401(k) Beneficiaries

Pensions, IRAs, and 401(k)s are paid to the named beneficiary of
your account, not the beneficiary stated in your will. Pensions
and 401(k)s have an added complication because by federal law
your spouse is your beneficiary. Even if you have a pre-nuptial
agreement, will, or the plan's beneficiary form states a beneficiary who isn't your spouse, your money in your pension or
401(k) will go to your lawful spouse even if you're separated.
Your spouse must sign a waiver relinquishing the right to be the
beneficiary of your account in order for a non-spouse to be a
valid beneficiary.

For example, perhaps your will states your 401(k) is to go
to your children, not to your current spouse. Your 401(k) beneficiary form names your children as beneficiaries. You pass away.
Do your children receive your 401(k)? No, your current spouse
does. Why? Because by law, the beneficiary of a 401(k) is your
spouse. After your death, your spouse inherits your 401(k),
moves the money to an IRA or their own 401(k), then names his

or her children as the beneficiaries. Your children are completely by-passed. It doesn't matter what your will says.

IRAs Can Provide Better Estate Planning Solutions

IRAs are kind-of like 401(k)s that have grown up and left home. They aren't connected to an employer, and there is much more freedom with what you can do in them – including beneficiary and other estate options. When you leave an employer, you have the option of transferring your 401(k) money into an IRA account. Brokerages, banks, credit unions, etc., offer IRA accounts.

Estate planning with 401(k)s is an interesting proposition. On the one hand many of the regulations governing this area are written for qualified plans, including 401(k)s, but most of the estate planning training for financial professionals is concentrated on IRAs. The body of technical literature is sketchy on estate planning with 401(k)s, and what you can and can't do is foggier. Finding a knowledgeable estate attorney who specializes in IRAs is hard enough, but trying to find one knowledgeable in estate planning with 401(k)s can be very difficult. Because of this, it's easier to do estate planning with an IRA, than a 401(k).

If you move your 401(k) money into an IRA, you can give your beneficiaries the option of a payout period stretched over many years. This way taxes are kept to a minimum. Be

aware, however, that if you don't have a trust as the main
beneficiary of your IRA, through which your beneficiaries will
receive their inheritance from your IRA, then there is no control
of how much the beneficiaries take out. If the beneficiaries don't
care about a big tax bite, they can take it all, and like a flash, it's
gone. If you want to control how and when your beneficiaries
receive your money, then you need to consider having a trust
created. A trust is a legal instrument that can control the
distribution of your money after your death. You can have a
trust set up so your money is distributed in a variety of ways.
For instance, you can dribble it out to your beneficiaries a little
bit every year, or give it to them all at once when they reach a
certain age. (Refer to the last section of Chapter 8 for help
locating a specialized estate planning attorney.)

Some Plans Allow In-Service Distributions

There are a small number of 401(k) plans that allow participants
to remove their money from the plan while they are still employed by the sponsor of the plan. Some plans allow you to
remove all of your money at almost any time (rare), and some
have restrictions on the distributions. If you have a difficult
estate planning problem, and it would be better to have the
planning options more easily available in an IRA, then find out
if there is an in-service distribution option for your plan.

A large employer in my area of the state has several
401(k) plans that allow in-service distributions. Two of the

plans allow in-service distributions of all the money at age 59½, another allows only removal of a portion at age 59½, while yet another allows a group of employees that entered the company through a merger to remove most of their money from the former employer's 401(k). Most participants in these plans don't know these options are available and few take advantage of them.

If you have this option available in your plan, and you decide to move your money to an IRA, make sure you find a caring, competent financial advisor to either manage the money for you, or assist you in the investment selection. DO NOT use this option as an opportunity to learn investing. I have heard numerous stories of people, who thought investing was easy, tried to learn with their retirement money, and ended up losing most of it. Be very careful.

Document All Your Retirement Plans

It's important to be careful, as the following story shows.

Pat of Raskob Kambourian Financial Advisors told me recently, "We had a client pass away, and the widow asked us to attend the benefit review meeting with the HR department. We were there to verify that she would receive everything we had listed for her husband's various accounts with the company. It was a surprise to us when the amount the company said she would receive was going to be considerably less than we expected. We had his records with us, so we reviewed with

HR all the pieces of the payout we expected to be paid to her by the company. We showed HR the expected amounts of stock options, deferred comp, 401(k), pension, etc. As we reviewed our list with HR, we found they didn't have a significant piece of information due to a recent merger of the company. Once we showed HR the error, they corrected the record, and his widow received all she was due on a timely basis."

Make sure you keep with your will a list of all the retirement plans you are a participant in and a copy of the SPDs for each. Sometimes there is a death benefit, or there are various actions that need to be taken under these unfortunate circumstances in order to claim the account. If your beneficiaries don't have this information, they may never get all your money. For instance, if it's a former employer's plan that your family may not know exists, your account could go unclaimed.

One time I ordered the plan documents for a 401(k) plan from a large corporation with a vast bureaucracy. In due time the plan documents arrived, and I began reviewing them. To my surprise, some poor and harried clerk had included a document that wasn't for public distribution along with the other copies I'd ordered. The document contained what appeared to be a list of participants of the 401(k) plan, complete with social security numbers, who were no longer employees, but had left their money in the plan. One account had under 50 cents in it, some had several hundred dollars, and a few contained thousands of dollars. I sat there and wondered how

many of these accounts were "lost" and would never be
claimed.

401(k) Quirks You Need to Know About

T hese are odd things about 401(k)s that can trip you up if
you're not careful. Most are rarely pointed out in 401(k)
books, but can have a significant impact on preserving your
money.

Loss of Control of Your Money

When you leave your 401(k) money with an employer after you
leave the company, you're losing the ability of knowing first-
hand what is happening with the retirement plan. Companies
are sold. Retirement plans are transferred. Plan custodians are
changed (as in the Enron situation). You may or may not be
kept informed. A group of Enron ex-employees claim they were
never informed about the "lockdown." Recently, a toll-free
number for a major employer's benefits line was changed without a recording giving the new telephone number. Anyone calling simply heard a recording stating it had been disconnected.

A nationally-known financial professional, famous for
his skill with retirement plans, has admitted he has lost track of
one of his former employer's retirement plans. The company

who sponsored the retirement plan was sold after he left the firm. The plan was moved, causing him great difficulty in tracking down his money and bagging it. If it can happen to him – it can happen to anybody.

A doctor told me one of his patients was seeing him because of psychological trauma associated with being laid-off. Already traumatized, the poor woman opened her mail one day to see her 401(k) account statement registering a big fat zero. All her money was gone! It took a frantic week of calls and searching before she located where her 401(k) money had been transferred.

I usually recommend to clients, if they leave their employer to take their 401(k) money with them. Transferring it to an IRA is a good option if you're already a skilled investor, or if you have a caring, competent financial professional. Another option is to move your money into the 401(k) plan of your new employer. Check out the new 401(k) carefully. Make sure it has a good selection of investment funds, and that it doesn't have any odd rules that will cause you difficulty.

The Problem with 401(k) Loans

If you have a 401(k) loan and you terminate your employment with the company sponsoring your 401(k) plan, the amount you still owe must immediately be paid. (Some 401(k)s allow a short grace period.) This is true no matter why you leave: new job, retirement or layoff. It doesn't matter. This can lead to very difficult situations.

I was assisting a woman who had been very successful with her employer and had made an excellent salary for many years as the primary money earner in her family. She was retirement age, and was furious that she was being laid off in a company downsizing. Unfortunately, she had indulged her children and herself for years, and had only a small 401(k) saved for retirement. The 401(k) had an outstanding loan, and if she left the company the amount she still owed on the loan would be deducted, seriously depleting the only savings she and her family had to live on. We discussed many options, including taking a lesser assignment in Vermont with her employer until she could pay back the loan. Finally, she defiantly refused to work in any way with her employer and left the company. She was so incensed with her employer that it blinded her to the destruction she was causing to her fragile finances.

Special Retirement Concerns

P eople's source of longing for retirement is as different as the people themselves. Some long for when they can finally do the things they've always wanted, and others desire to lay back and relax. Sam, a friend who is delighted to be retiring, exclaimed, "The shackles of corporate slavery are broken!"

Not long ago, retirement was a brief time period, but now with earlier retirement and longer, healthier lives, you can be retired longer than you were employed. Retiring at age 55 and living to age 95 means 40 years of retirement. This makes the decision about where to keep your retirement money very critical.

Here are some of the major difficulties 401(k) participants approaching retirement have to grapple with including whether to leave their money in the company 401(k) or not. This is a simplified overview of an extremely complex subject. For more exhaustive coverage of the subject, you'll find excellent books listed in "Appendix C: Additional Resources."

A Challenge to Your Organizational Skills

Art Linkletter once said, "Old age isn't for sissies." I'd like to add, "and retirement isn't for the organizationally-challenged." Once upon a time, people worked for one company, retired, and if they were fortunate, they received a pension. Now, when people retire they are looking at gathering in a hodgepodge of retirement plans from various employers. Our firm has been recently hired merely to organize all of the various retirement plans one person has. The nit-picky details of each plan, let alone trying to coordinate the whole kit and caboodle of them, is a confusing morass to most people.

One of the clients we are assisting with retirement organizing has a total of eight retirement plans from *one em-*

ployer in the categories of traditional pensions, cash balance pensions, 401(k)s, and 401(a)s. All of them have different rules and payout formulas. He isn't a manager or executive with his company. If he were, he would have even more.

An added bonus of moving your 401(k) to an IRA is the opportunity to simplify your life by consolidating many employer retirement plan accounts into one IRA. If you have eight retirement plans, then in most cases, they can go into one IRA.

Please don't feel like there is something wrong if you feel overwhelmed with all the details of retirement. You're not alone. Many people feel the same way.

Retiring or Leaving Your Employer Between Ages 55 - 59½

Age 55 is an important dividing line for 401(k) plans. If you stop working for the employer who is the plan sponsor before you reach the day you turn age 55, then you can leave your money in that 401(k) plan, but you can't take penalty-free distributions from it until you turn age 59½. If you leave the day you turn age 55 or later, you'll be able to leave your money in the plan and withdraw money from it without an early withdrawal penalty. You may be thinking, "Yeah, I wish I could retire at age 55." But various circumstances pop up that can make this rule very important to you.

Our firm assisted a couple in which one of them had unexpectedly inherited a condo in Florida. They were eager to leave corporate life behind and start their retirement. Due to various circumstances, the condo needed to have someone living in it soon. The wife volunteered to move there until the husband could join her. The problem was, she was age 54, not age 55. If she left her employer, she wouldn't be able to leave her 401(k) with her employer and make penalty-free withdrawals. She would only be able to remove all of her 401(k) money and move it to an IRA. The IRA withdrawal rules would bar her from making penalty-free withdrawals until age 59½. If she waited several more months until after she turned age 55 to leave her employer, she would be able to make penalty-free withdrawals from her 401(k) account to support their retirement.

A similar situation can occur if you're laid off before age 55 and need to access your 401(k) money. Sometimes you can negotiate when your lay off will begin. Some workers have been able to delay it for a few months, or have used accrued vacation time to stretch out their termination date in order to leave after they turn age 55.

There are three main options for 401(k) participants who leave their employer at or after age 55 and before age 59½.

1) Leave your money in your 401(k) and withdraw it as needed, penalty free. Once you reach age 55, then you can make penalty-free withdrawals from your employers' 401(k) plan. If your money was rolled over to an IRA you wouldn't be able to make penalty-free withdrawals until age 59½.

119

Be aware that if you discuss this option with a financial advisor, some advisors might be motivated to try and get you to move your money out of your 401(k) and into an IRA or annuity that he or she sells. Many advisors aren't aware of the advantages or disadvantages of leaving your money in a 401(k) until age 59½. They are simply taught how to transfer it out of a 401(k) and into their firm's investments.

2) **Leave the portion of your money in your 401(k) that you think you'll need between now and age 59½, and move the rest to an IRA.** This option allows you to withdraw needed funds from your 401(k) penalty-free, and allows you to have the advantages of better beneficiary and estate options, as well as more investment choices, for the portion in the IRA.

3) **Move your money to an IRA and create a "72(t)."** A "72(t)" is the informal name of an exception the IRS permits that allows you to avoid the 10% early withdrawal penalty if you take a distribution that is "part of a series of substantially equal payments." Essentially, the "72(t)" allows you to receive systematic distributions that must continue until you reach 59½, or until five years have passed, whichever occurs later.

The "72(t)" is an extremely complex exception. I can't emphasize enough the importance of working with a financial advisor who is experienced and knowledgeable with this method. Your advisor might have to hire an actuary to do the complex math involved in the creation of the "72(t)." When our firm creates these for clients, we explain that it's extremely

120

important for this method to be followed to the absolute letter of the law, or the 10% penalty will be charged on the total distribution. Despite the technicalities, the "72(t)" is a good way to have your money in an IRA, receive distributions, and avoid the 10% penalty while you're under 59½.

Your Plan Custodian Might Want Your Money

Plan custodians have become aware that some 401(k) participants are accumulating significant sums. Some custodians are trying to capture the management of these accounts for themselves rather than lose them to independent financial advisors or brokerage firms. When you mention to your plan's customer service representatives that you're retiring, you might be passed to a sales representative to convince you to remain with the custodian as an investment client. If you decide to have your plan custodian handle your 401(k) money, the custodian will move it out of your company's 401(k) and into an IRA.

The principles in Chapter 8 for selecting a financial advisor can help you decide if the plan custodian is a good choice to be your financial advisor. In addition, there are questions to ask yourself. Do you like dealing with a large bureaucracy? Would you rather have the personalized service of a small, independent financial advisor? On the other hand, if investments are your hobby, you might enjoy doing the investing yourself at a custodian such as Vanguard or Fidelity.

Limited Investment Choices

One of the characteristics of 401(k)s is that only a specific group of investments are offered to you. Some employers give a large selection of choices, such as Enron, which offered twenty. Some employers offer very few investment choices, such as a Fortune 500® company I know that offered only four until very recently. (Some plans offer a "self-managed option" that makes more investments available, but when you read Chapter 6 you learned why I don't recommend this option.)

The long and the short of it is, that when you're in a 401(k), you have limited investment options. If the plan administrator or plan custodian picks lousy investment choices for your plan – you're stuck with it. If you move your money into an IRA, then you can choose from a much wider selection of investment choices (certain regulations apply). If you have found a caring, competent financial advisor with a good track record, or if you're an experienced investor, then moving your money out of your 401(k), and into a larger universe of investment options in an IRA may be a good choice for you when you retire.

If you have little money, and know little about investing, keeping it in the 401(k) may be a better choice since the investment options are pre-screened for you. The investment choices are limited, which will help you to not feel overwhelmed.

A beautiful, hardworking, older woman who contacts me occasionally for help with her 401(k), looks far younger than her 70 + years. She knows little about investing, but she is an amazing woman who works full time and is determined to keep right on working. Fortunately, she has a job she enjoys.

Through various circumstances, she has been unable to accumulate a lot for retirement. She doesn't have enough to qualify for the investment minimum most financial professionals require to manage an investment portfolio. I have counseled her to keep her money in her 401(k) even if she has to retire. I've also recommended she move a former employer's 401(k) from a rollover IRA, where it was languishing, into her 401(k). I've explained to her that her money would be safer in her 401(k), where her investment choices are limited, but good, than in an IRA where her investment choices are more diverse, but overwhelming. An added bonus, is that she has someone who knows her plan and can help her select her 401(k) investments.

Your Company Might Require Immediate Removal of Your Money

Some employers demand that employees remove their money immediately from the plan when they retire. This can create havoc in the retiree's life as he or she frantically tries to find a financial advisor to assist them on short notice. In the situations I have helped with, the employers involved didn't handle the situations well. The human resource departments were quite blunt, unsympathetic, and the very short deadline, unyielding. Read your plan's SPD and talk to your plan's customer service center to find out whether your employer permits you to leave your money in the company's 401(k). You don't want a nasty surprise.

One man was abruptly laid off just before the holidays and told he had to have his money out of the company plans prior to New Year's Day. I remember struggling to get the proper paperwork from the company, setting up an IRA to receive it, processing multiple required documents, and taking care of numerous other details, all during the holidays on a short deadline. It was an experience I won't soon forget!

Age 70½ Pay Outs

A little known provision of some retirement plans is that when you reach age 70½, there will be an automatic payout of the entire account. If your plan has this provision, then you won't be able to leave your money in the plan during your later retirement years. The SPD for your plan should state if your plan contains this or a similar provision.

I've counseled 401(k) participants who were bound and determined to keep their money in their 401(k) after retirement. Sometimes I've delivered the unpleasant news that one of their retirement plans has a 70½ payout. They always have the oddest look of shock on their faces as though they've been hit on the head with a baseball from out of nowhere. They've spent years planning their retirement, but they didn't know to check to make sure the plan could do what they wanted.

Be aware that different retirement plans at the same employer might have different rules. For instance, a large aerospace contractor has five retirement plans that are 401(k)s, or something similar, assigned to various employee groupings. Of the five, two have age 70½ automatic payout; the rest don't.

It's important to let your financial advisor know if your 401(k) plan has an odd rule such as this.

Your Company Might Not Let You Remove Your Money until a Certain Age

Make sure you read your 401(k) plan's SPD to find out the restrictions on when you can receive your money. You don't want to spend years planning for an early retirement, then at the last minute find out you can't access your money until a later date.

Difficulty in Finding a Financial Advisor To Assist You

If you would like to leave your money in your company's 401(k) during your retirement rather than move it to an IRA, then you may have trouble finding a financial advisor who will be able to advise you during retirement. Many excellent financial advisors insist on having all your assets under their management in order to work with you as a client, and many aren't set up to manage money in a 401(k) plan. Also, many advisors are trained to help you get your money out of a 401(k), as opposed to helping you while you're in it. In Chapter 8, I'll discuss this difficulty in more detail.

8   SPECIALISTS TO PROTECT YOUR 401(K)

At first glance, managing your 401(k) may seem relatively simple. You put money in while you're working. You take money out when you retire. What could be more simple? Right? Well, it's a tad more complicated than that. In fact, it's a lot more complicated than that.

Lots of articles and books are written on 401(k)s. Can't those help? Well, yes, but most articles on 401(k)s either cover 401(k) legislation, investing, or give another sermon on diversifying. There are books that can help you with general knowledge about 401(k)s, and the literature from your company or plan custodian can help also. But what if you have a specific problem in your 401(k)? Perhaps your employer has made an error in how much it's matching in your account. Or, what if you get caught in a ground swell of emotion among your co-workers to own lots of company stock? How do you gain perspective? What about problems you don't know are problems? Problems that could result in lots of taxes or your beneficiaries never getting your money?

ENRON PROOF YOUR 401(K)

It's important for you to have specialists you can turn to who can help you achieve 401(k) success. There are three types of specialists you need to help you with your 401(k).

A 401(k) Specialist

K eep your eyes out for a 401(k) specialist in your local area. Specialists who assist 401(k) participants with problems while they are in the plans are tough to find.

A while back, the employer of one of my clients fouled up and didn't put in my client's 401(k) contributions for a few months. When my client discovered the error, the employer fought putting the money back. At the time, I was unsure of how to handle the situation. I called a person who is nationally famous for her work with qualified plans, which include 401(k)s. I explained the problem, and she quickly determined it was outside of her field of expertise. She has extensive knowledge of other qualified plan specialists, and cited a number of prominent individuals. Finally she came to the conclusion that none of them specialized in helping people get their money into plans, only out of it.

I was never able to find anyone to assist my client, but the experience helped me realize that there are few specialists who assist clients while they are in their plans. There are many who are eager to assist when people are leaving their plans, because that is when advisors make money. It was an illuminating experience for me. Since then, helping people solve 401(k) problems while they are in their 401(k) plans has become one of my specialities (the other is assisting people in getting the full amount due them from their pension).

Most specialists in qualified plans specialize in distributions from the plans or setting up the plans for corporations. There are, however, a few avenues available to you for help.

If you're fortunate, there may be an advisor who specializes in your employer's retirement plans. Building a niche by exclusively servicing one or two giant corporations is a small, but growing trend. An advisor selects a large, local corporation, and intensively studies the 401(k), pension, stock option, and other benefit plans the corporation offers. He or she becomes the expert employees can turn to for impartial advice. The advisor isn't associated in any way with the corporation; he or she simply services the employees as a means of building up his or her practice.

Around the country, here and there, the trend is growing. Two financial professionals in California have built a network of advisors in various parts of the country who specialize in the retirement plans of specific telecom companies. In another part of the country, an advisor has a thriving practice exclusively devoted to Merck employees. In Bethesda, Maryland an advisor devotes his energies to serving Marriott employees. Our firm is the only firm we are aware of specializing in the retirement plans of Lockheed Martin.

You have a great advantage if you're seeking 401(k) advice from a firm specializing in your company. When a Lockheed Martin employee meets with me, I already know his or her benefits, 401(k) pay out methods, pensions, and many subtle details that can cause difficulties. Ask your co-workers and managers if they know of a financial professional specializing in your company's retirement plans, but still be very careful because some investment product salespeople use niches as a ploy.

There are some excellent professional 401(k) educators who are paid by corporations to conduct workshops for the employees. Some of these individuals know a lot about 401(k)s and might help if you have a problem. Others just know their presentation materials, and some aren't licensed to give advice.

Don't confuse these professional educators with the advisors who do free workshops at lunchtime or after work. These advisors are doing workshops to locate individuals who will invest their 401(k) when they leave the company. Some of them are caring, competent financial professionals and some are investment product salespeople. If you think you might like to hire one of these advisors, work through the items in the next section to see if he or she is a good fit for you.

Fortunately, a caring, competent financial professional doesn't need to be a 401(k) expert to steer you away from an Enron-style disaster. An advisor might not know how to resolve problems in your 401(k), but a competent financial professional can quickly see if you have too much company stock in your 401(k) or help you develop a good plan for your overall financial situation. Help from someone like this would have dramatically reduced Enron employees' losses.

A Professional Coach for Your 401(k)

H iring a financial professional to assist you can be one of the most important decisions of your life. A wrong selection can be a set back, but a right decision can propel you forward to financial freedom. There are some excellent financial professionals out there. This section will help you ferret out a good one to meet your specialized needs.

Types of Financial Advisors

The most general term bandied about is "financial advisor." This is a moniker applied to just about anyone in the financial advisory field who provides advice. The truth is there are only four types of advisors in the financial advisory field: investment product salespeople; investment product salespeople masquerading as caring and competent financial professionals; advisors who are truly caring and competent financial professionals; and, highly specialized financial professionals.

The investment product salesperson has the goal of making money by selling you products: mutual funds, stocks, limited partnerships, annuities, and even financial plans. They move from one customer sale to the next trying to keep the money rolling in. The pressure is always on. Sales quotas must be met. It's a real grind. Many investment product salespeople are on this treadmill because they were trained by their companies to think this way and the company's system of compensation encourages it. But let's be frank, some of them joined the profession because they thought there was big money to be made. Some who join for this reason, leave after a few years when they realize what incredibly hard work this profession is. Others get in the groove of moving quickly from prospect to prospect in order to click off sales.

An unfortunate example of an investment product salesperson was an advisor who worked the investment desk at a local credit union associated with a large national corporation. Employees would do their banking, then buy investments. Because I am well-known to the employees of the corporation's local office, I would get irritated calls complaining about the performance of the investments this advisor had sold them and her lack of concern. People were confused why they weren't getting good service and wanted my impartial advice. They assumed their credit union would provide a caring, competent financial professional, but what they didn't realize is they were really dealing with an investment product salesperson. She simply recommended whatever the brokerage she was associated with told her to recommend that week, then went on to the next sale. When her customers saw their investments doing poorly and tried to discuss this with her; it might prod her to provide a little information. People were bewildered by her behavior, but once I clued them in, they began to understand.

The second type of financial advisor masquerades as a competent financial professional, but is in reality an investment product salesperson. This second type can have credentials and impressive schooling, but is still an investment product salesperson hustling a sale.

Some CPA's are acquiring the excellent AICPA/PFS designation that shows they are qualified in financial planning. No matter how excellent the designation, unfortunately, some bad apples turn up. I had just finished teaching a 401(k) workshop and was talking with one of the attendees who was probably in his late 40's or early 50's. He told me he had asked the CPA who did his taxes for advice about his 401(k) plan, and was told, "Why don't you just give that money to me to take care of?" I knew participants in his 401(k) plan couldn't remove any of their money until they reach age 59½ while they are employed by the company. From the way the man described the interaction with the CPA, it was evident the CPA didn't understand most 401(k)s don't allow distributions before the person leaves the company, nor had the CPA tried to acquaint himself with the details of his client's 401(k) plan. He just wanted that money to put into an investment product that would earn him a commission.

A doctor I know confessed how worried she was about her investment advisor. She explained the advisor had impressive credentials including a master's degree in financial planning, but the doctor had also noted the professional's expensive imported sports car and the very expensive investments the advisor was recommending. The doctor exclaimed, "I'm afraid I'm my advisor's next car payment!" Investment product sales people come in many different disguises.

Keep in mind that simply because an advisor says they are a "financial planner" doesn't mean they aren't an investment product salesperson. Selling financial plans as a product to be hawked has become big business. In some big national firms, financial plans are a loss leader to get you in the door so you can be sold more investment products. The financial plans are often thick, important looking documents, but may not be very helpful.

The third type of financial advisor has the goal of providing wise advice and helping you build up your financial situation. They care about you, your situation, your goals, and your values. They want you to be successful. You have the feeling they are on your side coaching you to success and cheering you on. They are also technically superb at what they do.

The fourth type of financial advisor is a small sub-group who are highly specialized in one difficult aspect of finances. They have focused on an area other advisors touch on, but they have acquired technical skills to the point that they train advisors in the specialty, receive client referrals from advisors for the specialty, or write for consumer or professional publications about the specialty. This can happen in many areas such as college funding, long-term care insurance, and qualified plans.

By working through the information in this section during your search for a caring, competent financial advisor, you should be able to avoid investment product salespeople and those pretending they aren't investment product salespeople, but are. Title, credentials, and education don't really show you whether you're dealing with a salesperson or someone you want to hire. I've read items written by advisors who had all kinds of training and certifications, but dripped with greed. On the other hand, a hard-working advisor who doesn't have designations may be honest and straightforward and have the skills you need.

Do You Need a Financial Professional's Help?

It's very hard to pull the rip cord and sell large blocks of company stock to rebalance your 401(k) when everybody in the company is on the band wagon to buy more. One of the wisest men who every lived, King Solomon, said, "In an abundance of counselors is victory." Receiving impartial, third-party advice can be very helpful.

If you only want to get impartial, third-party advice about your investments in your 401(k), keep in mind most highly qualified and knowledgeable financial planners won't work on a piecemeal basis. They will want you to have a total financial plan done.

If you're in the rare situation of having a caring, competent financial professional in your area who specializes in your company's retirement plans, then it shouldn't be a problem to meet with him or her to discuss just your 401(k) investments. The advisor will do it frequently for other employees in your company. He or she will still want to review your entire financial situation so your 401(k) investments will fit into your overall goals and with your values. This is a responsible professional thing to do in order to make appropriate recommendations for you.

Perhaps you want more than 401(k) advice. Perhaps you want a financial plan that brings together all the pieces of your money puzzle into a unified plan. There is a wide spectrum of prices and types of plans. Ask questions and review sample plans before deciding which financial planner to hire.

The more complicated your situation, the more you need assistance. If you have stock options, are in a management deferred compensation plan, are within ten years of living on your retirement money, have a large amount of company stock, and so forth, find an advisor and pay the bucks to get help. Don't go it alone.

Work through the information in this section so you can discern which category an advisor or planner falls into. Be wise. Be careful. Be successful.

The Advisor's Sales Approach

Investment product salespeople will usually try to get you to buy based on fear. Caring and competent financial professionals don't put pressure on you.

Investment product salespeople will probe to find out how to sell you more. Caring and competent financial professionals will interview you to understand who you are, what your goals and values are, and to understand your total financial picture in order to determine how they can help you.

Investment product salespeople will be more interested in talking about their investment products, than they will be in understanding your needs. Caring and competent financial professionals will wait until they understand your situation, goals, and values before recommending actions.

The Advisor's Speciality

Many successful financial professionals primarily accept clients within specific specialties or niches.

Sometimes the niche is individuals who have more than a minimum net worth or a certain investment minimum. Don't be put off by this if you don't meet the criteria. It just means you have encountered someone who sets standards and is successful. Keep looking. Eventually, you'll find a good fit.

Some financial professionals concentrate on working with specific types of individuals. For instance, most advisors find working with engineers as clients very difficult. One advisor, a former engineer, has created a niche for himself by exclusively working with engineers. Financial professionals in his area are delighted to refer them to him.

There are financial firms that focus on segments of the population, such as Ronald Blue & Company, LLC which concentrates on the Christian market. Certain firms specialize in foreign nationals, and some meet the needs of individuals who live part of the year in Canada and part of the year in the U.S. Some financial professionals deal exclusively with military personnel. Sometimes firms have a speciality in working with complicated trusts and multi-generational wealth. Sometimes the specialty is comprehensive financial planning (an all inclusive type of financial planning).

There is a great advantage to working with a financial professional specializing in your need or your niche. Find out an advisor's specialty or niche by reviewing his or her Web site or literature, and interviewing the advisor on the telephone.

One of the keys to identifying an investment product salesperson is they will usually accept business from anyone. When you do initial telephone inquiries, ask the advisors their specialty, or the type of person who is a good fit for their practice. If someone hems and haws, doesn't have an answer, says that is not significant, or even, "Oh, I work with anyone," then you're probably talking with an investment product salesperson. Move on until you find an advisor with strong standards who knows how to meet your specific needs.

The Advisor's Experience in the World

Advising individuals about their financial situation is a multi-disciplinary profession. Having a profession prior to becoming a caring, competent financial professional is often an asset that adds depth to advice. It also can indicate the financial professional is doing what they love to do. Changing careers is difficult. Most people only do it if they really love what they are jumping into.

The Advisor's Compensation

There are four basic forms of compensation for an advisor: commissions, a commission and fee mix, fee-only, and lastly what I call "golden extras."

Commissions are paid to advisors when they sell investment products such as load mutual funds, limited partnerships, annuities, insurance, and similar items.

Commissions and fees is a common mix. This method of compensation is referred to as *fee-offset* or *fee-based*. The financial planner charges a fee for the completion of a financial plan, and then receives a commission if you purchase the recommended investment products.

Commissions can be useful for some people who have only a small amount to invest because many times caring, competent financial professionals can't make enough from a flat fee on a small account to properly service it.

You may be surprised by what is considered a small account. For some firms, it's accounts under $250,000, for others it's accounts under $100,000. The long hours to meet demands of government regulations, the hours needed to service an account, and the low fees for working with small accounts, make charging commissions for them the sensible option for many financial professionals.

Sometimes if you can get above a certain investment minimum your caring, competent financial professional can switch you to a fee-based system. Sometimes you can separately purchase the fee-based services such as hourly advice or financial planning.

The third means of compensation is *fee-only*, which involves no commission and compensation is strictly by fee. Fee-only can take many forms: a retainer (or flat fee), a project fee, an hourly fee, a percentage of income, or a percentage of assets. Since the financial professionals who are fee-only don't receive compensation from commissions, there isn't a bias to favor recommending certain investment products from particular companies because of the amount of advisor compensation. Fee-only financial professionals are estimated to be less than 20% of all financial advisors who advise consumers.

Some advisors call themselves fee-only, but still receive certain types of payments that pure fee-only advisors would refuse. It's not a show stopper if the advisor isn't pure fee-only. There are very good advisors who are compensated in other ways. In fact, there are many stockbrokers on commission who are fair in their recommendations. The problem is the system of commissions (and the prizes offered in this system) doesn't encourage delivering unbiased recommendations to the client.

Along that line, is the fourth area of compensation that I refer to as *golden extras*. An advisor can be paid for placing your account with a certain custodian, receive gifts for selling certain products, and even kickbacks from no-load mutual funds. I have seen ads in investment industry magazines offering fabulous vacations if only an advisor gets enough people to buy this or that investment. I even received an e-mail advertisement stating if I sold a certain annuity I'd get a Mercedes Benz! A small percentage of financial professionals, myself included, choose not to participate in these programs.

There is good news and bad news about advisor compensation and getting advice about your 401(k). The good news is that if you want an advisor to give you advice about your 401(k), there is no way for them to be biased by recommending an investment they can make money on. That is because most 401(k)s are a "closed shop." The investments in them are the only ones you can select (except for the self-managed option available in a minority of plans). The bad news is that because there is no way for an advisor to make money selling you an investment in your 401(k), then many advisors won't find the work attractive because you won't be buying any investment products. If you want to hire someone to coach you to 401(k) success, you'll either need to find a fee-only, or fee-based planner who will accept hourly fees to give you advice, or who will do a financial plan for a fee.

The way to find out how an advisor is compensated is to read his or her ADV. It's a form an investment advisor must fill out and keep up-to-date that gives detailed information about compensation and other matters. The form is filed by the investment advisory firm with either the state securities board or the SEC. Investment advisors are required to give you a copy of a portion of the ADV, called ADV Part II. In it is a detailed account of how the advisory firm, and therefore the advisors at the firm, receive compensation. It's dull, dry, ultra-boring reading, but give it a mind-numbing chance.

The ADV forms are in the process of being placed on the Web so you can access them easily. Eventually, you'll be able to scan a number of ADVs to help you pare down your list of advisors to consider hiring. Information on how to access the ADVs already on the Web is listed in Appendix C in the section on checking advisors' backgrounds.

The Advisor's Approach to Working with You

Advisors vary in their approach to working with clients. Some work directly with you. Some assign your case to an assistant. Ask an advisor if you'll work directly with them. If you'll be assigned to an associate, then meet the associate to see if you want to work with that person.

There really is no key, based on an advisor's approach to working with a client, to help you discern whether you're talking with an investment product salesperson or a caring, competent advisor.

The Advisor's Credentials and Memberships

I deeply respect the incredible amount of effort individuals put forth to obtain the top-level credentials in the financial advisory field. While many credentials and memberships can show the person's depth of training, it unfortunately doesn't reveal whether a person is an investment product salesperson-in-hiding or a caring, competent financial professional. Some advisors have impressive credentials and are technically very proficient, but I wouldn't trust them with my money. Some advisors lack impressive credentials, but provide good service and are trustworthy.

What an advisor's credentials or memberships can give you is a peek into either how the advisor works or what they might have foc used on earlier in their career. Membership in NAPFA means the financial planner does pure fee-only, comprehensive financial planning. AICPA/PFS means the advisor was originally trained as a CPA. The certifications CLU and ChFC means the advisor probably started his or her professional life in the insurance field. CFA indicates the advisor's focus is more than likely investments as opposed to other specialties.

Certifications and memberships indicating specialization in 401(k)s are few and far between. The emphasis in the financial services industry has been on extracting a participants' money out of 401(k) plans, and there has been little emphasis, or monetary reward, in assisting 401(k) participants with their day-to-day problems. Most of the training in the industry that doesn't focus on distributions from the plans, is for advisors who set up retirement plans for corporations. The Chartered Retirement Plans Specialist (CRPS) focuses on 401(k)s, IRAs, pensions, and non-qualified retirement plans. Few have this credential, and most who do are involved in setting up plans. Having a membership in the Profit Sharing/401(k) Council of America can indicate a specialization in 401(k)s.

The Advisor's Investment Philosophy

Financial advisors come in a spectrum of investment philosophies. One end of the spectrum is rigid asset allocation; the other is market timing. They are polar opposites.

Rigid asset allocation in its most basic form is placing a little bit of your investments in a wide variety of different types of investments (called asset classes) so you cut the chances of losing a lot in any one type of investment. You won't get rich this way, but you're usually not going to end up penniless either. You select the investments once, and you don't touch them for years. This type of investing plugs away year after year (hopefully) making steady progress.

During the late 1990s when stocks were growing like crazy, many clients of financial professionals who used rigid asset allocation became very frustrated because this investment philosophy doesn't lend itself to rapid growth. Clients left only to be zapped by the stock market dropping like a rock in the years 2000 through 2002, giving those planners the last laugh.

As a side note, over the last few years the fundamental research on which rigid asset allocation is built, has been challenged as seriously flawed. You'll find passionate proponents on both sides of the debate.

The opposite investment philosophy, market timing, is much more active than rigid asset allocation. A financial professional tries to discern what the market is currently doing and where it may be going. Certain areas of the U.S. stock market go up or down depending on where the American economic cycle is at any point in time. A market timer buys or sells based on this knowledge.

Some financial professionals use a modified asset allocation model with a dash of market timing. Some use market timing with a dash of asset allocation.

Which investment philosophy is best in a 401(k)? That is hard to answer. Some of it depends on what you're comfortable with, and some of it depends on how close you are to retirement.

401(k)s are set up in such a way that pure market timing is very hard to execute in a 401(k) account. Pure market timing uses lots of buys and sells, and is very sensitive to what the market is currently doing. You would either have to be a very sophisticated, successful investor focusing on the stock markets constantly, or you'd have to have a money manager handling the account for you (an option in only a few plans).

A modified form of market timing does work in 401(k) accounts. We use this with our 401(k) clients and the approach works well. You have to have an advisor who understands the specific investments in your 401(k) and who will issue investment instructions at the right time to buy or sell. Sometimes we keep the same recommendations for over a year, but when the investments need to change, it's important to do it promptly.

Financial advisors whose investment style is market timing with an emphasis on almost daily buying and selling stocks (rather than mutual funds) will probably not be a good pick as your advisor. These types of advisors can be good working with money outside of your 401(k) if you have some money you want to take a risk with, but it's just not practical in your 401(k). This type of advisor can be good at what they do, but usually find it dull to sort through bland, 401(k) mutual fund investments. If you're interviewing an advisor, and they talk excitedly about how much money they've made for their clients by frequently moving them in and out of investments in hot, hot, hot stocks – move on to the next advisor.

When you interview advisors ask if they use rigid asset allocation or market timing. Caring, competent professionals tend to be passionate about the subject. If the financial professional you're talking to just smooths over the subject, or tries to lure you in with stories of mammoth returns for clients, then you're probably talking to an investment product salesperson.

The Advisor's Background

Checking an advisor's background requires two types of checking. The first involves checking to see if the advisor has been in trouble with securities regulators or if investors have filed complaints. The second is double-checking the advisor's credentials. These two steps are vitally important to avoid con artists, bad advisors, or disreputable firms.

For both types of checking, make sure you have the advisor's full name and the address where he or she is doing business. In addition, when checking for regulatory problems or investor complaints, you'll need the firm's full name where the advisor works. Financial planners might be either stockbrokers, investment advisors, or both. Contact information for the organizations below are in Appendix C.

For checking the background of stockbrokers, go to the National Association of Securities Dealers (NASD) Web site or call their toll-free number. More information might be available from your state securities regulation office.

For checking the background of investment advisors (almost any financial professional paid to give advice about investing in securities) go to the Investment Advisor Public

Disclosure (IAPD) Web site, or contact the Security and Exchange Commission's office of Public Reference. Not all investment advisors are listed on the IAPD system yet, which is currently being completed. Give your state securities regulations office a call to get information on investment advisors not in the IAPD.

Let me point out, however, that errors can happen. I received a call from a woman who immediately began quizzing me about our firm with a tone of heavy suspicion. Puzzled by this, I asked what prompted her call. "Well, my aunt got this flier on her door knob for your seminar next week, and I want to know who you people really are," she shot back. I explained we weren't doing any seminars next week, and we didn't advertise with door knob fliers. "What company are you calling?" I inquired. She said, "Retirement Specialists," – the name of our firm. She had obtained our toll-free number from a national telephone service. Now, I was really perplexed. Finally, it dawned on me, "Where are you calling from?" "California," she flatly answered. "Ma'm, we're in Texas. We don't do business in California." Bewildered, she stammered, "Then why is your company's name on this flier?" I explained, "Because companies are incorporated by their state, and the company in California simply has the same name our firm does." Embarrassed, she hung up.

On the other hand, I discovered one day that I had a call on my home answering machine from an advisor who said he had guaranteed investments that brought in great returns. An alarm bell went off in my mind since advisors aren't allowed to guarantee results. Curious, I jotted down his name and began researching his background. I searched the NASD's database to see if he was a stockbroker. Nothing. I called the Texas State Securities Board to see if he was a financial advisor or planner. Nothing. Then I checked the fraud department of the Texas State Securities Board. Bingo. This "advisor" had been convicted of fraud and had lost his license. The fraud investigator I spoke with said, "Thank you for calling. We are verrrrry interested in him." I think he'll be making future calls from the slammer.

A growing problem is credential fraud. Underhanded individuals claim they are CFP® professionals or have graduated from prestigious college programs in financial planning. The key to uncovering bogus credentials is contacting the regulatory bodies governing the credential or contacting the schools. For CFP® professionals, go to the CFP Board's Web site. For the CLU or ChFC designations, call the American College in Bryn Mawr, Pennsylvania.

Does the Advisor Want to Help You Achieve What Is Important to You?

Caring, competent financial professionals listen to your needs and your values, then help you with an action plan to get you to where you want to go.

149

Earlier in the book, I mentioned Derek V. Irish, a CFP® professional and client manager for Ronald Blue & Co., LLC, who helped an Enron employee rescue 90% of her Enron 401(k) and corporate compensation. He developed a financial plan supporting what was important to her. Derek explained, "With her there were other values that came into play other than money. She valued very highly that, if anything happened to her, then her widowed mom would have a good nest egg. When I heard what was important to her, this made an impact on how I built her portfolio. It's important the advisor takes time to understand the client's situation and what is deeply valuable to them as a person. I could have done a risk assessment and just given her an asset allocation for her 401(k). This, however, wouldn't have provided as good a solution as taking the time to understand what her values and priorities were, and thinking through how that needed to be factored into the recommendation."

The opposite approach is the investment product salesperson who will shmooze with you to get a sale, then move to their next target.

Does the Advisor Know 401(k)s ?

Qualified plans are one of the most intricate areas of government regulations. These plans are governed by a mammoth number of rules. One of the top technical books on the area admits it probably contains errors since the topic is so complex.

Some financial professionals are excellent with comprehensive financial planning, but aren't specialists in qualified plans. Keep in mind that you're looking for a financial professional you can have a long-term professional relationship with who will be able to help you as issues with your 401(k) come up over time. There are even some 401(k) issues that hide below the surface, and unless a financial professional knows to inquire about them, you or your beneficiaries could get into trouble.

I greatly appreciate the vast knowledge and skill CFP® professionals and other top-level certifications represent. However, keep in mind that unless the financial professional has specifically applied themselves to the specialty of 401(k)s, their knowledge will probably be limited to assisting you with plan distributions and over age 70½ minimum distributions. Most will regard your 401(k) as a piece of the larger puzzle of your financial situation. Few are even aware of the many and distinct dangers 401(k) participants face while they are active in their plans.

The upper-level credentials in the financial advisory field such as CFP®, AICPA/PFS, CFA, ChFC, and so forth, indicate an advisor has a broad array of valuable technical skills. The credential, however, doesn't necessarily indicate a significant knowledge base in 401(k) issues. For instance, out of fifteen pages listing topics the CFP Board states a CFP® professional must be competent in, 401(k)s along with other retirement plans are represented in only 6 out of 101 topics.

It's rare to find an advisor who specializes in 401(k)s, but you can find advisors who have studied qualified plan distributions. The question to ask an advisor is, "What do you think of the work of Natalie Choate or Seymour Goldberg?" If the advisor doesn't know who these prominent people are who train advisors in this highly technical area, then move on to another advisor. If the advisor thinks highly of them, then ask what's interesting about this type of work to him or her. Try to get them to talk. (You can ask, "What do you think of Natalie Choate's book, *Life and Death Planning for Retirement Benefits*?" If they pull it off their book shelf and talk excitedly about it, that is a very good sign.) Inquire about how he or she uses this specialized information in their practice. You should be able to discern if the advisor is genuinely interested in this type of work.

One strong clue to indicate you're dealing with an investment product salesperson and not a concerned, competent financial professional is that a salesperson will rarely take a genuine interest in your 401(k), want to understand the investments in it, and your goals for it. They often view 401(k) investment advice as a throw-away type of item to attract you to their office so they can sell you an investment product.

An advisor doing telemarketing just happened to reach me on my home telephone. He gave me his sales spiel, not knowing I was a 401(k) specialist. For some odd reason, I was curious as to how he would respond to 401(k) questions. At the time, my husband had a 401(k) at a large, local employer. I explained this to the advisor, and asked if he was familiar with this plan. He became quite excited when he realized there was a lump of money and assured me he could obtain the information about this plan by a circuitous route involving contacts from cocktail parties. He assured me he knew 401(k)s, but the more he talked, the more he revealed how little he knew. What he did know was how desperately he wanted to get me into his office, and if knowing 401(k)s would do it, then he knew 401(k)s.

Another example was a couple who visited a financial advisor at their financial institution for advice about the investments to choose in the husband's 401(k). The advisor gave them a quick recommendation for the 401(k), then advised them to open IRAs and buy some of the investment products he sold. The couple sensed something was wrong. Because they knew one of the specialties of our firm was the 401(k) the husband was in, they met with us. We reviewed the advisor's recommendations, which were poor for this particular 401(k) plan and for the couple, and made appropriate recommendations.

Chemistry with the Advisor

Caring, competent financial professionals really want YOU to succeed. It's what really turns them on. Investment product salespeople's hearts beat faster at the thought of MONEY.

When you're in the presence of a caring, competent financial professional, you feel respected. You start feeling like you can really make it to your goals.

Many investment product salespeople have been taught to use fear and intimidation as a sales tool. But beware! Some of the slickest investment product salespeople can make you feel like you're the center of the world. The ones who are true scam artists are masters of this. Read any article about financial advisors who turned out to be rip-off artists, and repeatedly you'll read comments like, "He was so good with people," "He made me feel so important," "He was the nicest man."

Recently, I listened to a person near retirement tell me what an enjoyable meeting he had with two representatives of a prominent financial firm. He met with them in his home to discuss investing his 401(k) and pension with their firm. He was touched by how much interest the representatives showed in his family. By the person's description of the conversation, I knew what the representatives were doing. Their company sells long-term care insurance, and they were patiently weaseling their way through family information to see if they could sell the insurance. Fortunately, since the firm had a terrible reputation, he made the decision not to entrust his retirement money to them. Even though this man is excellent in a profession that requires careful, analytical decision-making, these two representatives were so skilled at developing "chemistry" they almost induced him to make a very poor choice.

"Chemistry" is the number one element leading people to the wrong advisor. Only if an advisor meets the other requirements listed in this section should you consider "chemistry." Be careful about relying on your emotions to choose an advisor. Find a person who is honest, straightforward and technically competent. You're not adopting them into your family. You're going to meet a few times a year, and their technical expertise is going to help you become financially sound and successful.

Searching for an Advisor

One of the best ways to find a caring, competent financial professional is to ask financially successful people you know for the name of their financial advisor. Although this often produces a good result, sometimes it doesn't.

We have a hard-working, older woman who turned to us for advice about her pension and her 401(k), after previously going to an advisor her supervisor recommended to her. Years after meeting with the advisor, she is still incensed by his treatment of her. She bought what the advisor recommended, but she vowed never to go back again – and didn't. The type of person she met with was an investment product salesperson who had wealthy trappings and did lots of advertising. The moral of the story is that even with referrals, you still need to work through all the items I've listed to determine if you really want to work with a particular financial professional.

If you don't know anyone to ask, then go to the NAPFA, CFP Board, or Financial Planning Association (FPA) Web sites for referrals to local professionals who meet these organizations' criteria. The sites have helpful tips as well as Web-based tools to assist you with your search.

A Technical Specialist to Protect Your 401(k)

I f something happens to you, what would happen to your 401(k)? Do you have a young child to provide for? If your beneficiary inherited the full amount all at once, would it devastate him or her? If you're in a second marriage, do you want your children to receive your 401(k) money instead of your current spouse? What if your children are minors? Or mentally-challenged?

Your caring, competent financial professional should be able to help with these problems. In some cases the expertise of an estate attorney is also needed. Estate attorneys write wills and trusts, and generally make sure your money goes where you intend after you pass on.

Find an estate attorney to give you advice who specializes in estate planning involving qualified plans. The reason it's important for you to work with a specialist is that some of the standard language that estate attorneys use in writing trusts will result in difficulties for your beneficiaries if it's used in a trust document involving a qualified plan. There are generally only a handful (or less) in an entire state who are specialists in working with qualified plans.

How in the world, you may ask, am I ever going to find an estate attorney like that? If you've worked through each step of finding a caring, competent financial professional and have hired an excellent one, then your task should be easy. He or she should already have a relationship developed with a highly specialized estate attorney.

If your advisor doesn't have a relationship with one, then try the following. Usually these types of attorneys are in demand as speakers for the local financial professional associations such as FPA or AICPA/PFS. If you go to these organizations' Web sites or call the national offices (listed in Appendix C) you should be able to contact the local chapter. Ask the local chapter if an estate attorney specializing in qualified retirement plans has spoken to the group in the last year. If the answer is "yes," then jot down the name and contact him or her. If the answer is "no," then ask who in this part of the state is well-known for this type of work. Often there will be someone who is prominent.

When you call, ask the attorney similar questions as those recommended for determining if a financial professional knows qualified plans. "What do you think of the work of Natalie Choate or Seymour Goldberg?" is good to ask. If the attorney isn't aware of these individuals, or doesn't think highly of them, this is a red flag.

Estate attorneys can be expensive, so make sure you ask questions before agreeing to an appointment. Sometimes you can find one who has reasonable fees. Our firm refers clients to an estate attorney who is well-known in our area of the state for her expertise in qualified plans. She has free initial consultations, and quotes fees up front.

Perhaps you've already had a trust document created by an estate attorney. If your trust involves your 401(k), be safe and have it reviewed by a highly specialized estate attorney who works with qualified plans.

9   YOUR 401(K)
PROTECTION ACTION
PLAN

Your 401(k) money is very important to you, and the fact you're reading this book shows your strong desire to protect your money and make good decisions about it. Bravo! Let's look at the steps you need to take in order for your desire to become a reality. I can't promise these steps will keep your 401(k) money out of all danger, but I can tell you that if you do each one of these items, you'll dramatically increase your chances of protecting your 401(k) money and provide for a good retirement.

Gaining Insights Into Your 401(k)

401(k)s are complicated. It's easy to feel overwhelmed by all the governmental regulations, and also your 401(k) plan's bureaucracy. There are significant benefits to learning about your plan, and not letting it intimidate you. At first it will seem like a monstrous task, but if you take it a step at a time, I think you'll find that it's something you can do. The SPD is usually the easiest of the plan documents to understand. Sometimes they are even illustrated with cartoons and are a lot of fun to read. The plan document is usually very technical, but if you focus on the few sections you need to understand, then you should do fine. If you joined your present company because your previous employer was bought by, or merged with your current company, then be on the lookout in the SPD or plan document for special rules and provisions that may cover you.

❑   **Make files to organize all your 401(k) information.**
Refer to the end of Chapter 6 for the list of files.

❑   **Order an SPD for your 401(k) plan.**
If you have an SPD for your 401(k), call the plan's customer service telephone number and ask if it's the latest and greatest version. If it isn't, or if you don't have an SPD for the plan, then order one. Don't give up if you don't get it on the first try. Be persistent.

❑   **Order the Summary of Material Modifications (SMM) and the plan document.**

Where to write for them is in the SPD (often at the back). There is a sample letter to help you in "Appendix A: Ordering Your 401(k) Plan's Information."

❑ **Find a quiet place to read your SPD, the SMMs, and certain sections of the plan document.**

Lay the SPD and plan document side by side and compare the sections on contributions and distributions. Read the SMMs. Seek help from a knowledgeable financial advisor if it doesn't make sense.

❑ **Is your 401(k) actually more than one plan? Does it have an ESOP? Are there any others?**

Taking Action with Company Stock

I f you're allowed to sell your company stock, then use the checklist below. If you aren't allowed yet to sell your company stock, then use the checklist in the section, "If You're Still Restricted from Selling Your Company Stock," which follows the section below, and lists additional steps for you to take.

If You're No Longer Restricted from Selling Your Company Stock

❑ Find out when you're allowed to sell your company stock.

Look in your SPD. Check the SMMs. Look in your plan document's table of contents and read the section on when participants can sell company stock. Since the laws in this area are changing, call the customer service number for your 401(k) plan and ask what the current rule is for your plan.

❑ Learn how to buy and sell investments in your 401(k).

Other than wrestling with your company to get all your plan information, this has the potential for being the most frustrating of the steps you'll do. Stick with it because this is one of the MOST important things to learn to help you keep your money safe.

❑ Sell your company stock until you're within the limit of 5% to 12% of your 401(k) account.

Although some advisors allow a client to have up to 20% to 25% of their account in company stock, I

162

personally believe this is too high. Please talk with a caring, competent financial advisor to determine the appropriate percentage you should own. *Please Note: The company stock price might go up in value after you sell your company stock.*

❑   ## Diversify the investments you own in your 401(k) account.

Use "Appendix B: 401(k) Investment Diversification Help" to assist you. For further help, ask for assistance from a caring, competent financial advisor.

❑   ## Rebalance your account periodically.

Different 401(k)s have different rules about how often you may buy and sell investments. Read your SPD and find out what the rules are in your plan.

A good rule of thumb is to check your 401(k) account every three to six months to see if any of your investments have grown or gone down enough to have caused you to have too much of any one investment. If your company match is paid in company stock, then it's especially important to keep rebalancing your account by selling your company stock to keep it within the recommended limits. (Some 401(k) plans pay the company match in cash, not stock.)

❏ If you're near retirement, make sure you don't have more than 5% to 12% of your 401(k) account in company stock.
Diversifying your account is very important since you're near retirement.

❏ Don't leave your money in a difficult to manage or an out-of-favor retirement plan if you're allowed to move your money out.
Remember the troubles the Enron employees had with the ESOP.

If You're Still Restricted from Selling Your Company Stock

Here are some additional steps for you to take if you're restricted from selling your company stock. Also do the steps that you can in the section above, such as learning how to buy and sell investments and diversifying your account.

❏ If you can't sell your company stock to get the percent below the 5% to 12% limits, at least don't buy more.

If you think that you have a good reason to own more, then please discuss this with a caring, competent financial advisor.

❏ Try to save more to make up for the fact that a portion of your 401(k) account is in danger because it's in company stock you can't sell.

First, make sure you're contributing enough to your 401(k) to receive the maximum employer contribution. After that, make sure you have a three to six month emergency fund saved in your checking or savings account. If you have this set aside, then save for your next purchase, such as a car or house. When you have these items taken care of, then max out your IRA for the year. After this, try to contribute the maximum to your 401(k). I recommend that you discuss your situation with a financial advisor, and he or she can adjust these recommendations.

Making Sure You're Not Ripped Off

4 01(k) plans are very complicated, and it's easy for an error to occur. In addition to this, it's not uncommon for plan

representatives to give out inaccurate information. You have to remain alert and vigilant to protect your money.

❑ Learn how to read your pay stub, so you know if your contribution is going in your 401(k) account.

Try to find a person in your company's payroll or accounting department who will explain the codes on your pay stub.

❑ Call your plan's customer service number and ask one of the representatives to help you understand your 401(k) account statement.

If the first person you speak with isn't helpful, then call back again and again until you find someone who is. Sometimes I've had to call a plan's customer service line three or four times to get someone who is knowledgeable about something I've needed to know. Stick with it. Your 401(k) account statement gives you information that helps you know how to protect your money.

❑ Whenever you ask your 401(k) plan for important information, write down the representative's full name, the date, the time, and what they said. File it in the appropriate 401(k) folder.

Rounding Up Former Employer 401(k)s

I have found that most people have a scattering of plans here and there that have been left with old employers. That is one of the best ways I know to lose your money. I recently had a wonderful couple come to me, and hire me to organize their search for all their former and current employer retirement plans and to coordinate getting information on each. They are being smart. This is a very important thing to do.

❑ List all of your former employers and the retirement plans at each. Make plans to consolidate them, so you can take good care of them.

Most retirement plans can be moved to an IRA after you leave the employer. If you can't move the plan to an IRA, then at least make sure you keep the former employer informed of your new address. Make sure you have an SPD for each of your former employer plans. Check the SPD before you try to move the plan because sometimes there is a reduced payout if you receive your money before retirement. I recommend you get the help of a caring, competent financial advisor to help you move the plans, because errors can cost you penalties and taxes.

Making Sure Your Loved Ones Aren't Cheated

The rules for estate planning with 401(k)s and other retirement plans are very complex. With some areas of 401(k)s, you can read instructions and figure out what you need to do. When it comes to your beneficiary designations and coordinating them with your will, property ownership, and so forth, just give up and get help from a professional advisor!

❏   Fill out new beneficiary forms for your plan and file them with your company. For helpful tips see Chapters 6 and 7 under the appropriate sections.

❏   Read the last section in Chapter 8, "A Technical Specialist to Protect Your 401(k)."

If you're in a situation similar to the situations listed in the last section of Chapter 8, talk with a financial advisor about your situation and determine if you need to meet with a highly specialized estate attorney.

❑ Make sure your beneficiary selection in your 401(k) plans, your will, and other items are all in order so your beneficiaries won't have to worry.

Work with your caring, competent financial advisor (and highly specialized estate attorney if needed). This is a complicated legal area. Make sure you get good advice.

Finding a Professional Coach

Finding a great financial advisor to be your coach can really put you on track to protecting your 401(k) and accomplishing your retirement dreams.

❑ If you work for a large corporation, the military, or for the government in a central location (such as a state capital or Washington, D.C.), then ask financially

successful co-workers if there is a financial advisor who specializes in your company's or institution's retirement plans.

❏ Ask financially successful friends who
they use as a financial advisor.

❏ Take time to think through what type of
advisor that you would like to have.

For instance, if you're a young professional, would you
like to work with a firm that specializes in that niche,
rather than a firm that primarily serves retirees? Or,
perhaps investing is your hobby, but you would like a
fee-only advisor to consult on areas that you don't
know, such as beneficiary designations.

❏ Interview financial advisors.

For helpful tips on selecting an appropriate advisor,
refer to Chapter 8.

❏ Check advisors' backgrounds.

Refer to the appropriate section in Chapter 8 for how to
do this. The contact information is in Appendix C.

❏   Select an advisor to be your 401(k) and
       financial coach.

Gather your financial data, and your 401(k) plan data in
preparation for meeting with your new advisor.

Other Items to Be Done

A s you've read this book, several things have probably occurred to you to do to protect your money. Perhaps your
memory has been jogged, or maybe there is something that
you've been meaning to do, but just haven't done yet.

A woman called, and asked if I could help her obtain
her money from a former employer. She had left the money in
the plan when she stopped working for the employer, thinking
it would be safe. Now years had passed, and she was unsure
where her money was, especially since the employer wouldn't
answer her letters. Unfortunately, she soon was distracted with
a new project, and dropped the effort to retrieve her money.
The sad truth is, she may never see that retirement money
again. Don't let this happen to you.

On the next page, you'll find an action item list for you
to jot down things to do to protect your 401(k). Even if you can
only accomplish one item a month, you will be making progress. You worked hard for your money. You deserve to keep it.

Action Items

1. _____

2. _____

3. _____

4. _____

5. _____

6. _____

7. _____

8. _____

9. _____

APPENDIXES

APPENDIX A
ORDERING YOUR 401(K)
PLAN'S INFORMATION

R eading the plan documents is one of the most important things you can do to be able to make good decisions that will protect your money. Getting your plan's documents from your company, however, can be a challenge. Some companies are terrific about supplying the documents quickly, some are very slow, and some make it very difficult to get your plan information. Below is a letter to use to request your plan's documents.

Tip #1: To find out the formal name of your plan, look on the top of your 401(k) account statement. Or, if you already have an SPD for the plan, it should be in there.

Tip #2: The plan is allowed to charge you a reasonable fee for the information it sends you. Find out the charge before you send the letter, and include the amount as a check or money order. The SPD is free.

Tip #3: To find out the address for where to send the letter, look in the SPD for your plan. If you don't have an SPD, then call the customer service line for your plan and ask. Sometimes the customer service representatives don't know the address. If that is the case, call the department in charge of the retirement plans for your company.

Tip #4: Type your name just below your signature.

The Letter

To Whom It May Concern:

I am researching the retirement plans that I have been in or am now covered by while I have been employed by (name of your employer). I am requesting information on the following plan (state the formal name of the plan you're in). I would like to receive for this plan:

1) A copy of the current, available IRS 5500 form for this plan.

2) Any Summaries of Material Modification if there have been changes to the plan.

3) A Summary Plan Description

4) A copy of the Plan Document

I understand that the price of the plan document is (the price your company charges), and I have included a (check or money order) for (the amount) to cover what I have ordered.

Please send the above items to:

(Your address)

Thank you. I appreciate your help.

Sincerely,

(Your signature)

(Type your full name below your signature.)

(Your social security number or employee identification number should be typed here.)

APPENDIX B
401(k) INVESTMENT
DIVERSIFICATION HELP

H ere is some information to assist you in achieving a simple form of diversification in your 401(k).

The two charts below can help you diversify your 401(k) investments. Use the "Types of Stock Mutual Funds" chart with the stock mutual funds and company stock in your 401(k). Use the "Types of Bond Mutual Funds" chart with the bond mutual funds in your 401(k). Ask a knowledgeable financial professional, an experienced investor, or refer to *Morningstar Reports* to determine the appropriate quadrant for your 401(k) plan's investment funds and company stock. By choosing investments which are in different quadrants, you can achieve a simple form of diversification.

There are two types of mutual funds in 401(k)s: retail and institutional. *Retail mutual funds* are like going to Walmart – there are lots of choices that have been advertised heavily to the public and tons of competition between brands for your dollar. You can follow the investing ups and downs of these funds either in the newspaper or at Web sites such as Yahoo!Finance.

With *institutional funds* on the other hand, it's almost impossible for the average investor to ferret out information on them. Don't waste your time trying to find them in the newspaper. Institutional funds are a big boys game – one of the publications that publishes information about these funds has a subscription cost of $2,500 per year.

Morningstar is a reporting service that can be very helpful to you. Its reports are available in most library reference departments, and many financial professionals also have the information. Any of your mutual fund selections which are retail mutual funds should be listed in the *Morningstar Reports* at the library, or at the *Morningstar* Web site (www.morningstar.com). *Morningstar Reports* will show what quadrant the retail funds are in. Unfortunately, many 401(k) funds are "institutional only" funds, which aren't covered by *Morningstar* in their public reports. Check your plan's Web site, or call the plan's customer service center, to see if your plan offers *Morningstar's* institutional fund reports for institutional funds in your 401(k).

Types of Stock Mutual Funds

Value	Growth	
		Large Company
		Small Company

Types of Bond Mutual Funds

	Low Risk	High Risk	
			Long Maturity
			Short Maturity

APPENDIX C
ADDITIONAL
RESOURCES

Information on 401(k)s

Books

David Wray, *Take Control with Your 401(k): An Employee's Guide to Maximizing Your Investments* (Dearborn Trade, 2002).

Twila Slesnick, Ph.D, Enrolled Agent, and Attorney John C. Suttle, CPA, *IRAs, 401(k)s & Other Retirement Plans* (Berkeley: Nolo). Nolo books are updated regularly. Ask for the most recent edition.

Ralph Warner, *Get a Life: You Don't Need a Million to Retire Well* (Berkeley, Nolo). Nolo books are updated regularly. Ask for the most recent edition.

Wayne G. Bogosian and Dee Lee, *The Complete Idiot's Guide to 401(k) Plans* (Indianapolis: Macmillan Publishing, 2002).

401(k) Plan Document Information

To obtain free and unlimited Internet access to the IRS 5500 forms your employer files on its 401(k) plans (if it's in the freeERISA.com database): http://www.freeERISA.com

USLaw.com

Covers many different topics including 401(k) withdrawal rules: http://www.uslaw.com/vsimplify/401k.htm

401kHelpCenter.com

Lots of helpful information. Free weekly newsletter available listing new 401(k) articles on the Web: http://www.401khelpcenter.com

U.S. Department of Labor

A hit list of the top ten warning signs for trouble in your company's 401(k) plan: http://www.dol.gov/dol/pwba/public/pubs/protect/guide10.htm

Information on Estate Planning

Denis Clifford & Cora Jordan, *Plan Your Estate: Absolutely Everything You Need to Know to Protect Your Loved Ones* (Berkeley: Nolo). Nolo books are updated regularly. Ask for the most recent edition.

Information On Beginning the Financial Planning Process and Finding a Financial Advisor

Bill Bachrach, *Values-Based Financial Planning™: The Art of Creating an Inspiring Financial Strategy* (San Diego: Aim High Publishing, 2000).

Information on How to Get Out of Debt and Get on Track Financially

Dave Ramsey is a syndicated, national radio talk show host who specializes in helping people get out of debt and become financially secure. He has excellent materials to help you develop a budget and make good financial decisions. You can find his materials, and the national schedule for his radio show at: http://www.DaveRamsey.com

Information on Enron

401(k) Participants' Lawsuit Against Enron
http://www.enronerisa.com

To Assist the 401(k) Participant's Lawsuit with any Information Pertinent to the Case:
http://www.enronerisa.com/case.html

To Read the Enron 401(k) Participants' Consolidated Lawsuit:
http://www.enronerisa.com/pdf/Enron1stConsolidatedAmende
dComplaint.pdf

Information on Top Management Buying or Selling Company Stock

To see if top management personnel are buying or selling
simply go to: http://finance.yahoo.com/quotes?symbols. Enter
the symbol for your company's stock in the left entry box. In
the right entry box, click on "Research" in the pull down menu.
Click "Get." In the "More Info" menu bar click "Insiders."
Scroll down to see whether management insiders are buying or
selling.

Investment Software

Peter Worden put out a warning on Enron stock in the summer
of 2001. To learn more about the investment software that he
offers: http://www.TC2000.com.

To Check the Background of a Financial Professional

Securities and Exchange Commission
On this Web page you'll find good information for researching
the background of an advisor, and there are links to help you do

it. Also there is a link on this page to help you find your state securities regulator: http://www.sec.gov/investor/brokers.htm

Or, you can call or write:
Securities and Exchange Commission
Office of Public Reference
450 5ᵗʰ Street, NW, Room 1300
Washington, D.C. 20549-0102
Phone: 202/942-8090
Fax: 202/628-9001
E-mail: publicinfo@sec.gov

Investment Advisor Public Disclosure (IAPD)
Web site to see financial advisors' ADVs:
http://www.adviserinfo.sec.gov/IAPD/Content/lapdMain/iapd_SiteMap.asp

NASD
Also try the National Association of Securities Dealers online search: http://www.NASDR.com/2001.asp. Or you can call the NASD at 800/289-9999.

To Double-Check Credentials or Help With Locating a Financial Professional

For CFP® Professionals:
CFP® stands for "Certified Financial Planner."

Certified Financial Planner Board of Standards, Inc.

1700 Broadway, Suite 2100

Denver, CO 80290-2101

Phone: 888/237-6275

Fax: 303/860-7388

Web Site: http://www.CFP-Board.org

E-mail: mail@CFP-Board.org

For CLU or ChFC:

CLU stands for "Chartered Life Underwriter."

ChFC stands for "Chartered Financial Consultant."

The American College

270 S. Bryn Mawr Ave.

Bryn Mawr, PA 19010

Phone: 610/526-1000

Web Site: http://www.amercoll.edu

NAPFA

National Association of Personal Financial Advisors

355 West Dundee Road, Suite 200

Buffalo Grove, Illinois 60089

Phone: 800/366-2732

Fax: 847/537-7740

Web Site: http://www.napfa.org

E-mail: info@napfa.org

AICPA/PFS

Unfortunately, there appears to be no direct help on AICPA's Web site to help you check a PFS credential or locate a CPA with this designation. Try the office below for assistance in checking the advisor's credential.

American Institute of Certified Public Accountants
1211 Avenue of the Americas
New York, New York 10036-8775
Phone: 212/596-6200
Fax: 212/596-6213
Web Site: http://www.AICPA.org

Financial Planning Association (FPA)

FPA has set up a National Planning Support Center to help consumers select CFP® professionals. When you go to the FPA Web site, toward the bottom of the menu on the left of the page is "Planner Search." Click on it to locate a CFP® professional.

FPA/Atlanta Office
5775 Glenridge Drive, NE Suite B-300
Atlanta, Georgia 30328
Phone: 800/647-6340
Fax: 404/845-3660
Web Site: http://www.fpanet.org
E-mail: supportcenter@fpanet.org

ABOUT THE AUTHOR

CRISTA F. BOYLES is one of the founders of Retirement Specialists Incorporated, a fee-only investment advisory firm in Houston, Texas that concentrates in the areas of assisting consumers with their 401(k) problems, qualified plan distributions, and investment portfolio management. Crista serves as vice president of the firm's consumer 401(k) and pension services.

Crista's practice includes a special emphasis in obtaining full benefits for plan participants. She is actively involved in technical advice and consulting to plan participants, interpreting plan documents, investigating benefit accuracy, and employer benefit error resolution. Crista has obtained thousands of additional dollars for plan participants.

She speaks on how plan participants can obtain their full benefits in 401(k)s and pensions. She conducts workshops to assist plan participants manage their 401(k) accounts and writes a monthly column, *The 401(k) & Pension Coach* ™. She is a member of the Financial Planning Association (FPA) and the Profit Sharing/401(k) Council of America.

Crista has appeared on talk shows to promote consumer financial safety, and her comments have appeared in *Reader's Digest*.

NOTES

In citing works in the notes, short titles have generally been used. Refer to the bibliography for the full citation.

GENERAL NOTES:
A. In an attempt to make the information on 401(k)s less technical and more readable, I have chosen to use the word "employees" in many places where, to be technically accurate, the word should be "participants."

B. Details of the personal stories have been changed to protect the privacy of the individuals involved, unless permission was obtained.

C. All endnotes are in the same order as the material in the text of the chapter.

CHAPTER 1
ENRON'S NEW ACCOUNTING METHOD
   The method Enron began to use in 1991 is referred to as, "mark-to-market," accounting.
   Flashbacks, *Forbes*.
CAROL COALE
   Ivanovich, "The Fall of Enron / Enron: How Could It Go So Wrong So Fast?"
1999 VIDEO TAPED MEETING
   Reinert, "The Fall of Enron / Enron Exec's Testimony Disputed."
AUGUST 2000
   U.S. Senate, Robert Vigil, Testimony.
   Sixel, "Suit Alleges."

AUGUST 2000 (*continued*)
    Steffy, "How Enron Seduced."
2000 VIDEO TAPED MEETING
    Montgomery, "Lawmaker Points Finger."
JIM CHANOS INITAL STUDY
    Laing, "The Bear That Roared."
NELL MINOW SPEECH
    Machan, "I Am Watching."
END OF 2000 STOCK PRICE
    Tittle, et al. v. Enron Corp., et al.
CINDY OLSON SELLS
    Reinert, "The Fall of Enron / Enron Exec's Testimony."
ANALYSTS ON ENRON
    Laing, "The Bear That Roared."
    Holtzman, "Enron Chronology."
    Eavis, "Why One Firm Thinks."
SELECTION OF NEW TRUSTEE
    Enron, "Enron Explains Basic Facts."
    Kemper, et al. v. Enron Corp., et al.
DEALS GOING SOUR
    Berkowitz, "Video-On-Demand."
    Public Citizen, "Liquid Assets."
    Laing, "The Bear That Roared."
SKILLING LEAVES
    AMI, "V.P. Cliff Baxter."
    BBC News, "Troubles Multiply."
    AMI, "A Letter from the Editor."
    Reuters, "Enron Reels."
SHERRON WATKINS' ALLEGATIONS
    AMI, "V.P. Sherron Watkins."
    CBS News, "The Paper Trail."
    Holtzman, "Enron Chronology."

SHERRON WATKINS' ALLEGATIONS (*continued*)
> Reinert, "The Fall of Enron / Execs Say They Tried."

UBS BROKER
> Ahrens, "Enron had Complained."

WATKINS AND LAY
> Rosen, "Exec Tells of Fear."

FASTOWS FURY AND INTIMIDATION
> Rosen, "Exec Tells of Fear."

AUGUST 23RD ANALYST DOWNGRADE
> Holtzman, "Enron Chronology."

LAY ANSWERS EMPLOYEE E-MAILS
> Reinert, "The Fall of Enron / Senator Suggests."

ELECTRONIC TOWN HALL MEETING AND WATKINS AN OFFICER
> Gottesdiener Law Firm, "The Kenneth Lay-Employee Town Hall."

SOME PORTLAND GENERAL ELECTRIC EMPLOYEES BARRED
> U.S. Senate, Robert Vigil, Testimony.

ENRON "LOCKDOWN" INITAL INFORMATION
> Enron, "Enron Explains Basic Facts."

VINSON & ELKINS REPORT BACK
> Schmidt, "Enron's Watkins Advised Lay."

THIRD QUARTER ANNOUNCEMENT AND EVENTS
> Steffy, "How Enron Seduced."
> Behr, "Enron Discloses."
> Earle, "Analysts Vent Anger."
> Staff, "Chronology."

DAVID DUNCAN SHREDDING
> CBS News, "The Paper Trail."

PERIOD RIGHT BEFORE THE "LOCKDOWN"
> Enron, "Enron Explains Basic Facts."

PAUL O'NEILL
> Joseph, "Enron Timeline: The Rise and Fall."

CREDIT RATING AGENCIES DOWNGRADE
Steffy, "How Enron Seduced."
RESTATE EARNINGS
La Monica, "Where Wall Street Went Wrong."
ROBERT RUBIN
Editorial, "Robert Rubin's Role."
DYNEGY
Behr, "Enron Accepts."
END OF "LOCKDOWN"
Enron, "Enron Explains Basic Facts."
Keller Rohrback LLP's Enron ERISA fraud site.
FIFTEEN STOCK ANALYSTS AND CNNMONEY
La Monica, "Where Wall Street Went Wrong."
DEFERRED COMPENSATION PARTICIPANT
Feldstein, "Enron's Retired Get Burned, Too."
PLAN ADMINISTRATOR OF DEFERRED COMPENSATION
Berger, "Deferred Payments."
JUNK BOND STATUS AND DYNEGY MERGER
La Monica, "Where Wall Street Went Wrong."
TRADING HALTED
BBC News, "Enron Fights for Life."
S&P 500® TERMINATION
La Monica, "Where Wall Street Went Wrong."
ENRON STOCK PRICE ON NOVEMBER 28TH
BBC News, "Enron Fights for Life."
RETENTION BONUSES
Public Citizen, "Chronology of Enron's Rise and Fall."
ENRON STOCK PRICE ON NOVEMBER 29TH
BBC News, "Enron 'to File for Bankruptcy.' "
LARGEST BANKRUPTCY AND ENERGY MARKETS SHUDDER
Steffy, "How Enron Seduced."
BANKRUPTCY TO BE HEARD IN NEW YORK
Goldberg, "Filing Seeks to Transfer."

CRIMINAL INVESTIGATION STARTED
    Robb, "Enron Timeline: The Rise and Fall."
TRADING HALTED
    CNN, "NYSE Drops Enron."
    Robb, "Enron Timeline: The Rise and Fall."
FASTOW DEATH THREATS
    Steffy, "How Enron Seduced."
    Ivanovich, "Center of the Storm."
3,000 FIRMS AND $5 BILLION
    Doward, "Enron's New $5bn Black Hole."
KEN LAY RESIGNS
    KPRC, "Lay Resigns from Enron Board."
    Public Citizen, "Chronology of Enron's Rise and Fall."
FAKE DEED TRANSFER
    Lezon, "Fake Transfer of Ownership."
EX-ENRON EMPLOYEES' SUIT, JANUARY 28TH
    Robb, "Enron Timeline: The Rise and Fall."
CINDY OLSON TESTIFIES
    Reinert, "The Fall of Enron / Enron Exec's Testimony."
EX-EMPLOYEE TESTIFIES ABOUT ENRON COLLAPSE
    Yost, "Enron Executives Plead 5th Amendment."
MIKIE RATH TESTIFIES
    Yost, "Enron Executives Plead 5th Amendment."
ANNOUNCEMENT SEEKING TO REPLACE TRUSTEES
    Strope, "Labor Dept. Seeks."
EX-EMPLOYEE COMMITTEE IN BANKRUPTCY
    Berger, "U.S. Trustee Panel."
STAY AGAINST ENRON LITIGATION LIFTED
    Ruiz, "Suits Against Enron."
ENRON PENSION PLAN UNDERFUNDED
    Associated Press, "Government Might Have to Take."
HUGE BONUSES PAID TO 2000 EXECUTIVES
    Eichenwald, "Enron Paid Huge Bonuses."

INDEPENDENT FIDUCIARY NAMED
Murphy, "Boston Company Named."
CONSOLIDATED COMPLAINT AGAINST BANKS
University of California Office of the President, "Banks,
Law Firms were Pivotal."
"DEAD PEASANT" POLICIES
Sixel, " 'Dead Peasant' Policies."
CINDY OLSON TO RESIGN
Staff, "Enron's Olson to Resign."
THE PLAY
Simonson, "Enron the Play."

CHAPTER 2
62% - 63% IN ENRON STOCK
Kemper, et al. v. Enron Corp., et al.
ENRON ESOP
Each employee participant actually had two accounts
within the Enron ESOP, but not wanting to bore you to
tears, I have simply avoided a detailed discussion of how
the Enron ESOP was set up. Only one of the two types of
accounts, the Retirement Subaccount, is part of the 401(k)
participants' consolidated lawsuit. The information about
the Enron ESOP in the book pertains to this account.
FIDUCIARY'S DUTIES
ERISA §404(a) (1) (B), 29 U.S.C. § 1104(a) (1) (B)
FIDUCIARY'S LOYALTY
ERISA §404(a) (1) (A), 29 U.S.C. § 1104(a) (1) (A)
SEARS ROEBUCK, CON EDISON, GM, FORD AND CITICORP
F.X.C. Investors Corp., "Our Recommended Guidelines."
TRAVIS FULLER
Fuller, e-mail to author.
ENRON EXECUTIVES NOT BEING ABLE TO SELL
Enron, "Enron Explains Basic Facts."

THE APPROPRIATENESS OF THE INVESTMENTS IN THE ENRON 401(K)
    Tittle, et al. v. Enron Corp., et al.
DAVID WRAY'S COMMENTS
    Wray, interview.
THE DETAILS ABOUT THE ENRON ESOP
    Tittle, et al. v. Enron Corp., et al.
THE ESTIMATE OF THE AVERAGE TOTAL LOSSES
    Kemper, et al. v. Enron Corp., et al.
NUMBER OF PARTICIPANTS IN THE PLAN
    Tittle, et al. v. Enron Corp., et al.

CHAPTER 3
    Tittle, et al. v. Enron Corp., et al.
ENRON EMPLOYEE WITH $600,000
    Irish, interview.
CLIENT UNDER AGE 50
    Middleton, e-mail to author.
ADAM
    Adam Drugid, e-mail to the *Houston Chronicle*.
11% OF ENRON STOCK IN COMPANY MATCH
    Tittle, et al. v. Enron Corp., et al.
FOUR ENRON EMPLOYEES
    Ferraresi, e-mail to author.
62%-63%
    Tittle, et al. v. Enron Corp., et al.
ENRON EMPLOYEE WHO HAD DIFFICULTY WITH MANAGER
    Reinert, "The Fall of Enron / Execs Say They Tried."
ENRON EMPLOYEES IN COLUMBUS, OHIO
    Hill, e-mail to author.

CHAPTER 4
S&P 500® AVERAGE RETURN FOR 1999 AND 1998, IN TABLE
    Browning, "Year-End Review."

S&P 500® AVERAGE RETURN FOR 2000, IN TABLE
>Bary, "Appropriately, 2000 Ends on a Downer."

S&P 500® AVERAGE RETURN FOR 2001, IN TABLE
>CitiStreet, "Capital Accumulation Plan."

EMPLOYEE #2'S COMMENTS
>AMI, "The Victims."

CHAPTER 5

"CERTAINLY AT A MINIMUM"
>Gleason, e-mail to author.

"COUNSELED SEVERAL"
>Hayes, e-mail to author.

PROCTER & GAMBLE EMPLOYEE
>Moody, e-mail to author.

WIFE PRIMARY EARNER
>Hammel, e-mail to author.

DIVERSIFY
>McNabb III, interview.

REBALANCE
>Wray, interview.

CHUCK'S LAW
>DiFalco, e-mail to author.

CHAPTER 6

YOUR COMPANY'S ESOP PLAN
>Rodrick, interview.

CHAPTER 7

PAT RASKOB
>Raskob, interview.

CHAPTER 8

LESS THAN 20% OF ALL ADVISORS ARE FEE-ONLY
>Bogosian, *The Complete Idiot's Guide to 401(k) Plans.*

BIBLIOGRAPHY

AMI. "A Letter from the Editor." *Inside Enron*, AMI Specials III, No. 3, 2002, p. 1.

AMI. "The Victims." *Inside Enron*, AMI Specials III, No. 3, 2002, p. 36.

AMI. "V.P. Cliff Baxter: Murder Disguised as Suicide?" *Inside Enron*, AMI Specials III, No. 3, 2002, p. 81.

AMI. "V.P. Sherron Watkins Alerts the Nation." *Inside Enron*, AMI Specials III, No. 3, 2002, p. 74.

Ahrens, Frank. "Enron had Complained about Fired Broker/UBS Employee Issued Warning on Stock." *Washington Post*, 27 March 2002, sec. A, p. 8.

Associated Press. "Government Might Have to Take Over Enron Pension Plan." *Houston Chronicle*, 28 February 2002, sec. Business, p. 6.

Bary, Andrew in The Trader. "Appropriately, 2000 Ends on a Downer." *Barron's*, 1 January 2001, p. MW3.

BBC News. "Enron Fights for Life After Bid Collapse." *BBCi*, 29 November 2001, sec. Business. 3 July 2002 (http://www.bbc.co.uk/business/)

BBC News. "Enron 'to File for Bankruptcy.' " *BBCi*, 30 November 2001, sec. Business. July 2002 (http://www.bbc.co.uk/business/)

BBC News. "Troubles Multiply at Enron." *BBCi*, 1 November 2001, sec. Business. July 2002 (http://www.bbc.co.uk/business/)

Behr, Peter. "Enron Accepts $8 Billion Buyout Offer From Dynegy." *Washington Post*, 10 November 2001, sec. E, p. 1.

Behr, Peter. "Enron Discloses SEC Inquiry." *Washington Post*, 23 October 2001, sec. E, p. 3.

Berger, Eric. "The Fall of Enron / Deferred Payments Under Fire / Hand-picked Group Cashed Out at Enron." *Houston Chronicle*, 17 August 2002, sec. C, p. 1, 7.

Berger, Eric. "U.S. Trustee Plans Panel to Represent Ex-workers." *Houston Chronicle*, 15 February 2002, sec. A, p. 24.

Berkowitz, Ben of Inside.com. "Video-On-Demand Stuck on Pause." *The Industry Standard*, 16 April 2001, sec. News From the Standard. 9 July 2002 (http://www.thestandard.com)

Bogosian, Wayne and Dee Lee. *The Complete Idiot's Guide to 401(k) Plans*, 2nd ed. Madison, Wisconsin: Alpha Books, 2002: 275.

Browning, E. S. "Year-End Review of Markets & Finance 1999: Stocks Approach the Stratosphere." *Wall Street Journal*. Jan. 3, 2000, sec. R, p. 1.

CBS News. "The Paper Trail." *CBSNews.com*, June 2002: Anderson Under Investigation. 1 July 2002 (http://www.cbsnews.com)

CitiStreet. "Capital Accumulation Plan Investment Results: Periods Ending December 31, 2001." CitiStreet reported to participants of the Lockheed Martin Capital Accumulation Plan in their quarterly account reports, Boston, 31 December 2001.

CNN. "NYSE Drops Enron; Andersen Drops Auditor." *CNN.com*, 15 January 2002, sec. Law. 3 July 2002 (http://www.cnn.com)

DiFalco, Chuck. E-mail to author. 18 July 2002.

Doward, Jamie. "Enron's New $5bn Black Hole." *The Observer*, 20 January 2002, sec. Business. 10 July 2002 (http://www.observer.co.uk/business)

Duguid, Adam. E-mail to the *Houston Chronicle*. December 4, 2001, sec. Enron Letters. July 2001 (http://www.HoustonChronicle.com)

Earle, Julie. "Analysts Vent Anger at 'Hidden' Enron Charge." *Financial Times*, 18 October 2001 (Updated October 22, 2001), sec. News & Analysis / Industries. 3 July 2002 (http://news.ft.com/home/us/)

Eavis, Peter. "Why One Firm Thinks Enron is Running Out of Gas." *TheStreet.com*, 9 May 2001, sec. Commentary. 3 July 2002 (http://www.TheStreet.com)

Editorial. "Robert Rubin's Role." *Washington Times*, 29 July 2002. 22 August 2002 (http://www.washtimes.com)

Eichenwald, Kurt. "Enron Paid Huge Bonuses in '01; Experts See a Motive for Cheating." *New York Times*, 1 March 2002, p. A1.

Enron. "Enron Explains Basic Facts About Its 401(k) Savings Plan." Enron, Enron Press Release, 12 December 2002.

Feldstein, Dan and Eric Berger. "Enron's Retired Get Burned, Too / Deferred-Salary Plan Fizzle." *Houston Chronicle*, 16 February 2002, sec. A, p. 1.

Ferraresi, Paul, CFP®. E-mail to author. 14 August 2002.

Flashbacks. *Forbes*, 18 March 2002, p. 54.

Fuller, Travis. E-mail to author. 28 July 2002.

F.X.C. Investors Corp., "Our Recommended Guidelines." For subscribers of FXCNewsletter.com. F.X.C. Investors Corp., 2002.

Gleason, Mark, CFA. E-mail to author. June 3, 2002.

Goldberg, Laura. "Filing Seeks to Transfer Enron Case to Houston." *Houston Chronicle* article reproduced on EnronErisa.com, 4 December 2001. July 2002 (http://www.EnronErisa.com)

Gottesdiener Law Firm. "The Kenneth Lay – Employee Town
Hall Meeting Transcript, September 26, 2001."
Gottesdiener Law Firm, Press Release, 18 January 2002.
Hammel, Richard K. CFP®. E-mail to author by Melissa
Hammel on behalf of Richard K. Hammel. 5 June 2002.
Hayes, Timothy. E-mail to author. 31 May 2002.
Hill, Adam, CFP®. E-mail to author. 20 August 2002.
Holtzman, Mark P. "Enron Chronology." *Enron Implosion Home
Page*. (date not indicated) Hofstra University. 10 July
2002 (http://people.hofstra.edu/faculty/Mark_P_
Holtzman/enron/Index2.htm)
Irish, Derek, CFP®. Telephone interview by author. 30 July 2002.
Ivanovich, David and Houston Chronicle Washington Bureau
Staff. "The Fall of Enron/Enron: How Could It Go so
Wrong so Fast?/Blame Laid on Lay, Large Investments."
Houston Chronicle, 2 December 2001, sec. A, p.1.
Ivanovich, David, Tom Fowler and Katherine Feser. "Center of
the Storm / Aggressive and Driven, Fastow has many
Faces." *Houston Chronicle*, 20 January 2002, sec. A, p. 1.
Keller Rohrback L.L.P's Enron ERISA fraud site, sec. Home page.
10 July 2002 (http://www.EnronErisa.com)
Kemper, et al. v. Enron Corp., et al., H-01-4089 (S.D. Tex.)
KPRC. "Lay Resigns from Enron Board." *KPRC*, 4 February
2002. July 2002 (http://www.Click2Houston.com)
Laing, Jonathan R. "The Bear That Roared: How Short-Seller
Jim Chanos Helped Expose Enron." *Barron's*, 28 January
2002, p. 18.
La Monica, Paul R. "Where Wall Street Went Wrong."
CNNMoney, 29 November 2001, sec. Personal Finance /
Investing. 3 July 2002 (http://money.cnn.com)
Lezon, Dale. "Fake Transfer of Ownership Filed for Lay
Properties." *Houston Chronicle*, 15 February 2002, sec. A,
p. 24.

Machan, Dyan. "I Am Watching." *Forbes*, 4 March 2002.

McNabb III, F. William. Interview by author, Houston, Texas. 19 March 2002.

Middleton, George, CFA, CPA/PFS. E-mail to author. 31 May 2002.

Montgomery, Dave. "Lawmaker Points Finger at Skilling for 2000 Talk." *Philadlphia Inquirer*, 26 February 2002, sec. US & World. 10 July 2002 (http://www.philly.com)

Moody, Rob, M.S., CFA, CFP®, CLU, ChFC. E-mail to author. 31 May 2002.

Murphy, Bill. "Boston Company Named to Oversee Employee Plans." *Houston Chronicle*, 15 March 2002, sec. Business, p. 5.

Public Citizen. "Chronology of Enron's Rise and Fall." *Public Citizen*, (date not indicated). 9 July 2002 (http://www.citizen.org)

Public Citizen. "Liquid Assets: Enron's Dip into Water Business Highlights Pitfalls of Privatization." *Public Citizen* (date not indicated), sec. Executive Summary. 9 July 2002 (http://www.citizen.org)

Raskob, Pat. Telephone interview by author. 5 June 2002.

Reuters. "Enron Reels as Heir-Apparent Skilling Exits." *The Industry Standard*, 15 August 2001, sec. News from the Wires. 9 July 2002 (http://www.thestandard.com)

Reinert, Patty. "The Fall of Enron / Execs Say They Tried to Protect Workers' Money." *Houston Chronicle*, 6 February 2002, sec. A, p. 13.

Reinert, Patty. "The Fall of Enron / Enron Exec's Testimony Disputed / Waxman says Tape Shows Olson Touted Firm's Stock." *Houston Chronicle*, 22 February 2002, sec. A, p. 10.

Reinert, Patty and Rosanna Ruiz. "The Fall of Enron / Senator Suggests Outside Firms for Retirement Plans / Leiberman Offers 401(k) Safeguards." *Houston Chronicle*, 12 February 2002, sec. A, p. 13.

Robb, Joseph. "Enron Timeline: The Rise and Fall of an Energy Giant." *The Sheridan Reporter*, 19 February 2002. 6 July 2002 (http://www.TheSheridanReporter.com)

Rodrick, Scott. Telephone interview by author. 31 January 2002.

Rosen, James of Bee's Washington Bureau. "Exec Tells of Fear at Enron." *Sacramento Bee*, 15 February 2002, sec. Politics. 2 July 2002 (http://www.sacbee.com)

Ruiz, Rosanna. "Suits Against Enron can Proceed / 401(k) Cases no Longer in Limbo." *Houston Chronicle*, 21 February 2002, sec. Business, p. 1.

Schmidt, Susan and David S. Hilzenrath. "Enron's Watkins Advised Lay on How to Blame Others." *Washington Post*, 14 February 2002, sec. Business/Energy, p. A02. 2 July 2002 (http://www.washingtonpost.com)

Simonson, Robert. "Enron the Play: MA's WHAT Stages Accounting Drama." *Playbill* on Yahoo!, 28 June 2002.

Sixel, L. M. "'Dead Peasant' Policies Benefit Top Executives." *Houston Chronicle*, 24 April 2002, sec. A, p. 1.

Sixel, L. M. "Suit Alleges Enron Led Workers Astray." *Houston Chronicle*, 23 November 2001, sec. Business, p. 1.

Steffy, Loren. "How Enron Seduced Wall Street: Andrew Fastow, Mystery CFO." *Bloomberg Markets*, January 2002. 10 July 2002 (http://www.bloomberg.com)

Staff. "Chronology." *Houston Chronicle*, 17 January 2002, sec. Enron - Nov. 2001. July 2002 (http://www.HoustonChronicle.com)

Staff. "Enron's Olson to Resign July 15." *Houston Chronicle*, June 28, 2002, sec. Business, p. 4.

Strope, Leigh of the Associated Press. "Labor Dept. Seeks to Replace Enron's 401(k) Executives." *Houston Chronicle,* 11 February 2002, sec. A, p. 4.

The Vanguard Group. *"The Vanguard Advantage."* 2002 edition, Valley Forge, Pennsylvania: The Vanguard Group, p. 13.

Tittle, et al. v. Enron Corp., et al., H-01-3913 (S.D. Tex.), 9-22, 56-63.

University of California Office of the President. "Banks, Law Firms were Pivotal in Executing Enron Securities Fraud." University of California News Release, 8 April 2002.

U.S. Senate. Robert Vigil testifying to the Committee on Commerce & Science Transportation. *Hearing on Enron.* 107th Congress, 1st session, 18 December 2001.

Wray, David. Telephone interview with author. 4 February 2002.

Yost, Pete. "Enron Executives Plead 5th Amendment." Associated Press on *Yahoo!News,* 7 February 2002. 20 July 2002 (http://dailynews.yahoo.com/)

INDEX